William Anderson Smith

Lewsiana

Or, Life in the Outer Hebrides

William Anderson Smith

Lewsiana
Or, Life in the Outer Hebrides

ISBN/EAN: 9783337315436

Printed in Europe, USA, Canada, Australia, Japan

Cover: Foto ©Andreas Hilbeck / pixelio.de

More available books at **www.hansebooks.com**

LEWSIANA

OR

LIFE IN THE OUTER HEBRIDES

By W. ANDERSON SMITH

AUTHOR OF "OFF THE CHAIN"

WITH ILLUSTRATIONS

LONDON
DALDY, ISBISTER, & CO.
56, LUDGATE HILL
1875

PREFACE.

A FEW of these descriptive papers appeared originally in the *Glasgow Herald*.

We have added an historical chapter from the best sources within our reach, but we claim no occult knowledge of the early ages.

If we have said aught to wound the suscepti-bilities of the "kindly Lews folk" it was far from our intention, as we have nothing but pleasant memories of the people and the land. May they all live to receive as much considera-tion as the deer and the grouse!

Nov., 1874.

THE HEBRIDEAN EXILE'S LAMENT
IN CANADA.

———◆———

Trees ! Trees! Trees!
   Sycamore, ash, and beech !
Oh ! for the wild sea-breeze
   That sweeps o'er the sandy reach.

Brushwood, tangled and green,
   Scrambles 'neath monarchs of oak ;
Far dearer to me the savage scene
   Where the sea-waves roll'd and broke.

Growth is heavy and rank :
   The earth is hard to reach :
Oh ! for the rocks where the blue-dove flocks
   O'er the wild sea-bitten beach.

Now snow lies deep around,
   And wolves are howling by ;
But I hear the surge that drown'd
   The low of the homely kye.

I hear the Barvas waves ˋ
  Thunder across the waste ;
I hear the wind that raves
  O'er the hut on the hillside placed.

Now the panting sun doth stand !
  And flowers rush up to heaven ;
Can I live in a choking land !
  My struggling heart seems riven !

Ye ships ! bear, bear me back !
  Ye winds ! beat 'gainst my brow !
Till Bernera's sunsets sink to black
  O'er the land I worship now.

CONTENTS.

LIST OF ILLUSTRATIONS.

HOW WE LIVED IN THE LEWS.

NOW you just pour the potatoes, and see that the fish is properly done, while we put on a fresh table-cover and set the table.—"Where will I pour them?"—Outside, round the corner; look about you, and see that you pour out the water, and keep the potatoes.—"Raining," you say! Of course it is raining! You would like to do as our native did, who poured the water down a rat's hole in his earthen floor, to save the lazy rascal twenty steps.

Well! now put on the pot again for a minute or two, while we throw out our note-book. Our linen-chest consists of a weekly supply of *Glasgow Heralds*, which are quite invaluable. First, as table-covers they require no washing; next, they are most convenient note-books when any "happy thoughts" strike one under the gentle stimulus of a cup of tea, or the solace of merry memories; and also they prove an ever-present literary attraction for the eye to wander over, perhaps to withdraw the mind from the occasional scantiness of the repast.

But this morning we cannot complain, for cod steaks fresh from the adjacent deep, and mealy potatoes from the neighbouring lazy-beds, are settled in their places by the cup that cheers. For here, as in Australia or Russia, a meal is not a meal without a potent bowl of tea. It seems a concomitant of semi-barbarism, for our teapot is never at rest, and already we have worn out two.

Hand over the loaf, please. Don't you suppose we want for bread, although twenty-five miles from a regular baker! Bread? Yes, the best of bread. This loaf is baked with sea-water, soured flour for yeast, and best American flour for sole ingredient. Cut and come again! There is no alum to spoil your teeth, you need not fear any internal objections, and you may eat it fresh from the pot with pleasure and impunity. "The pot?" Why, you don't expect we carry about a baker's oven! Mix smartly, knead thoroughly, drop it into the well-greased pot, and when it has risen, sink deep in the hot peat ashes.

Nothing like hot peat ashes for a cook, if you only properly appreciated them, ye Hebrideans! Do you wish to ramble off for a day, and come back to your lone apartment tired and hungry, but with hope still alive within you? Then pluck a pair of the fowls of the air—or water—stuff them nicely; say simply with bread crumbs, chopped onions, minced liver and gizzard, with plenty of salt and pepper; and lay on the bottom of the pot with a lump of suet for company. Now fill up with peeled potatoes, well spiced, and sink the closed pot in the hot ashes. Then be sure and bring a friend or two back to help you, unless you wish to be found playing boa-constrictor!

Hot peat ashes! "See how they run," like quicksilver. Just watch that heap, and you will understand all about the sounding sands of Jebel Nagus.

"All very fine," you say, "but what have we for dinner?" Hope, fresh air, and boundless possibilities. There are three hundred hooks on our spiller in the bay; but if we don't catch more than yesterday it won't be over-weighted. We had four hundred hooks out and only got one flounder—which can scarcely be called a fair return for some hundred molluscs, several hours of labour, and a fair allowance of really hard toil. Dinner? If we are in luck, then expect a fish pie; if feathers are about, trust in fried pigeons or an Irish stew.

Thou potent salmon-fisher! dost remember our Christmas stew? How the peats and the day were so damp, but your humour ever so dry; how your experienced camping-head made the most of the tag ends of vivres in that tag end of creation; and how merrily you taught our hands to cook and our fingers to fry?

But about our dinner? You *did* get dinner; but how many hours' stalking did it take to get that duck, "o'er muir and mire," while

you waited magnanimously "on spec"? You
old Californian camper-out, how you whipped
off the feathers, and neatly severed the joints,
and fried her, "cheek by jowl" with a golden
plover, till we felt for once as if we lived to
eat—and really what else do we? We are
savages for the nonce when provisions or
dainties run low, and the end-all and be-all of
our existence is to worship our domestic god.

Food! food! What shall we eat and what
shall we drink? That is the worst and the
best of exile from civilization. If you run out
here, you might as well be in Africa, so far
as the æsthetics of diet are concerned; and
we who ever ate what came, without consideration, have to consider much ere we can
eat at all.

Yet who could fear want of supplies, with
hospitality on either side, and Garynahine,
the large-hearted, within a "Sabbath day's
journey"? Alas, that the Grimersta and
Blackwater should know your rod no more;
that the sport you made and opened up to
others should be closed so ungraciously to

you! Can the Lews be the Lews without
you to the slayer of deer, the player of salmon?
A free-hearted Southerner should not go too
far North; an ever-warm hearth may thaw out
enemies!

But the northern day has passed, and we have
retired to our needed rest; when suddenly
"there is a sound of revelry by night," and
we are startled out of our first sleep by
oil-skinned apparitions who have been belated
on the deep, and now crowd about our peat fire
to light the calumet of peace. For no one
has more than a latch on the door in these
regions; and quite enough in general too.
Rarely did we turn the catch on the door,
and although articles of value to the fishermen
ever lay about in profusion, nothing whatever
was purloined. So general is the habit of open
doors at all hours, that we have heard of the
girls waking in the morning under their neighbours' blankets, which had been mischievously
exchanged by some larking youngsters during
the hours of darkness.

Well! friends! is the Carloway shore still

lonelier than of old, since there is no live peat
in the Dunan, and the smoke curls no longer
from the hearth of "the stranger"? Do you
ever miss a familiar face from the shores, or
a friendly participator as you "putt" the stone
beneath the well-known window? And you,
boys! you merry, intelligent, inquiring Celts!
do you miss the evening boxing-matches where
you had such fun; the shoals of *Illustrated News*
that repaid your willing assistance? We are
tired of you all; go away and herd your cattle,
poke about the pools for little fishes, or bring
us news of the whereabouts of the restless
doves!

"Were they ever troublesome?" you ask.
As well ask the careful housewife if " lady
callers" are always welcome; or a coal-pit
manager if his men are always pleased. Here is
a groan caught as it issued from the burdened
soul. It tells its own tale of woe :—

"Singularly free from sickness of all sorts,
considering their mode of life, there was yet
one epidemic of a most virulent character,
which at the time of our visit had laid violent

hands upon the usually healthy inhabitants of
the West. Not content with attacking and
fixing its poisoned fangs into the weakly and
the young, destroying their appetite for healthy
amusement, and causing them to rise hurriedly
from untasted tea, and turn contemptuously
from smoking suppers, it inserted its insidious
virus into the minds of the apparently sane
and vigorous, the sturdy fisherman, and lumber-
ing mechanic. Neither liberal Moderates, nor the
more constrained Free Churchman, could elude
its deadly influence; but young and old, rich
and poor, the comparatively wise and the
superlatively foolish, alike fell a prey to the
poisonous reptile that crept into their peaceful
homes, and drew the fascinated victims into
its deadly embrace!

"'Catch the Ten'* indeed! Catch the multitude! How often have we struggled in your
folds, you hideous reptile! 'Double dummy'
too, by all that's pathetic; for all had eaten of
the 'insane root that takes the reason prisoner,'

---

* Card game—called 'Scotch whist.'

the root of the tree of the knowledge of 'Catch the Ten.'

"Is it a wet winter morning, and you are chuckling on having a day to yourself amid the few books that the wilderness can furnish? Your simple breakfast has been cooked and disposed of, fresh peats are heaped on your little fire, the domesticities of a lonely bachelor, hermetizing, got over, and thanking that Providence that tempers the wind to the shorn lamb, and sends the rain to the student, you shake yourself, tome in hand, into a chair.

" A forenoon's quiet! don't you wish you may get it? Two forms darken the window, and the demon of 'Catch the Ten' lurks in their very step, and fanatical resolution in the twinkle of their eyes; can we not exorcise the evil spirit? Is it not possible to divert the channel of their thoughts for an hour or two? Not in the slightest! They are wholly possessed by it, and, willy nilly, you are drawn under the influence, and made to suffer for the sins of the people.

"Their good temper is imperturbable, their

resolution as immovable as their broad
shoulders; their appetite so insatiable, that
game after game only whets it the more, like
potatoes at dinner when they come from Wick.
How often have we wriggled in vain to escape
it, how often have we lied, how often insulted
our most esteemed friends: and all the time
they were possessed with the sublime idea
that they were kindly whiling away the hours
of idleness of a poor exile from civilization,
and all representations to the contrary were
regarded as arising from a delicacy on our
part in occupying *their* valuable time. Ah,
Job! Job! you might thank your Eastern
stars that your condoling friends never carried
a pack of cards, and played 'Catch the Ten'
on your cinder heap."

This is the luxury of complaint; the world
must grumble, and it is well, you say, when
we find our worst cause to do so, in the kind
hearts and easy laughing natures of those who
surround us. Is that so? Is it not rather
the truth that the "old men of the sea," who
sit upon the shoulders of struggling humanity,

are the easy-tempered, easy-going friends who accept all your efforts as their due, and cling affectionately round your neck until you sink exhausted under their selfish amiability. You good-for-nothing Celts, why are you so pleasant? How liberal and free you are, —what a strange mixture of the little and the great!

You never know how ignorant, impracticable, and helpless you are until thus set down at a distance from markets, away from the kind and skilful female hands that have hitherto ministered to your wants. Not a woman you could ask to cook a meal, or who could cook a pleasant meal if you could ask her; while, as for sewing a button on a shirt —— So, from feeling dependent, you become supremely confident in that dangerous thing, "a little knowledge," till, like the schoolmaster in "Adam Bede," you fancy woman ignorant of her simplest duties, and yourself fully competent to teach your mother to bake, your grandmother to spin, and your wife to darn stockings.

Feel lonely? never think of it. Whose

mind can harbour unrest with the lullaby of the sea at the door? who give way to despondency with the great ocean mother crooning their heart to rest?

"There is a rapture by the lonely shore,"

but it is the calm rapture in unison with the throbbing of the mighty heart of the universe, not the frantic frenzy that strives to emulate the little world that circles in the city. And if the receding tide does leave stagnation, if the time between the throbs is so great that man's little soul almost seems to cease between the mighty vibrations, is there no smaller world beside you to stir your little pulses? Turn up the seaweed of life beside you, see the robber crabs in their stolen dwellings, see crustacean meet crustacean in combat à outrance. No; there is no stagnation even here, but battle, murder, and sudden death. We have no fear of circulation ceasing, and seek not little signs of life. Rather will we lie on the sloping caps of the beautiful cliffs, and listen to the melodies of the mavis, forgetting that the music streams through a "valley of death," or view the circling peregrine ascend to its azure kingdom, nor remember that it, too, is but a sickle of the reaper.

Roughing it! forsooth, rather smoothing out our life; for rough indeed must "the world" ever appear to one who has laughed and lolled so long by the shores of the swinging Atlantic.

THE LEWS.

W HEN the name of the "The Lews" is mentioned, it rarely calls up any distinct idea in the minds of the public. A "peat floating in the Atlantic," it has been left outside, and, until lately, no one has held out a helping hand to draw it within our ken.

Since our first papers were printed, the West —our West—has been invaded by a charmed pen, and Sheila and Mairi, redolent of peat and heather, yet fresh as the Hebridean breezes, have been cajoled into saying "And are you ferry well?" to their southern neighbours. "And it's me that's glad" that they had a trip "whatever," for they don't see much company, and they have done us all good, and we are all "ferry proud and happy" to have met the Princess of Thule.

In the following pages we shall not attempt to introduce our readers to dames of high degree, but endeavour to show how the subjects of the Princess manage to exist.

As we have recently had particular opportunities of living among the cotters and fishermen in the most unfrequented district, and enjoyed the most intimate and friendly relations with all classes of the community, the result of our observations may not be uninteresting to the public.

Those questions most important to the sportsman have been recently so well handled by "Sixty-one" (Mr. Hutchison) that we shall confine ourselves principally to subjects of general interest. Men and manners in a barren land and a boisterous climate are surely worthy of at least a passing glance. The fact that they exist in happiness and comparative comfort, notwithstanding the gloomy aspect of nature, and hug their saturated peat moss as affectionately as if the sun of Italy were over them, and its fertile soil beneath, may point a moral to the growling multitude, surging

impatiently amid " a' the comforts o' the Saut-
market."

Let us suppose there has been a good year
for potatoes, what a work there is for the clergyman! The whole country-side is marrying, and
giving in marriage. In the year '71, not an
unmarried girl over eighteen was left in Shaddar,
and everywhere else it was on the same scale.
The potato crop did it. But before a Lews
young man can hope to make a good matri-
monial bargain he must go to the Wick fishing.
Once he has proved his manhood by bringing
back a few pounds from the everlasting Northern
herring harvest, he can calmly look around for
the girl that can carry the biggest creel of peat
across the moor, or the heaviest creel of seaweed
from the beach. Let him add to this a scrap of
a lot from the laird, or from the lot of his father,
and as soon as he has knocked up a hut, he is
a remarkably marriageable young man.

Formerly the cotters were much better off,
in a way, than at present; seeing they had
considerable-sized lots, where, with the labour
of their families and the manure supplied by

their cattle and the sea, they could raise enough to keep themselves in abundance, if not in luxury. But now population has increased to such an extent, without any proportionate increase in land allotted to them, and the lots have been so divided and subdivided, by the cotters themselves giving portions to their marrying sons or daughters, that few indeed now raise enough for their own necessities. They are thus forced to purchase meal or potatoes at the dearest season and in the dearest market.

It is a serious consideration whether the proprietor ought not to divide among these hordes some of the unlimited moor close by, or whether necessity will force them to emigrate, the solution hoped for by the laird, we fear in vain.

The erection of a dwelling-place, into which he may lead his partner in life, is not a very serious matter to a Lews man. No great skill is required, and little expense in materials, except for a few planks. The stones, everywhere abundant—for all through the West the rocks crop out amid the peat—are brought together,

and two rude walls built, one within the other,
all round. The interval between these two
walls, always several feet, sometimes many, is
filled up with earth and gravel, so as to form
one broad outer wall, only one door being considered necessary. Upon this wall the roof is
raised on a framework of old oars and odd
scraps of drift and other wood, an occasional
sound plank giving stability; these are again
covered over with "divots," or large turfs,
closely covering it, and these once more are
thatched over. The edge of the roof falls on
the inner corner of the outer wall, so as to
leave a broad top to the main wall all round.
This soon collects grass and plants, and is a
favourite promenade for the sheep of the establishment, as well as dogs and children. These
latter are the least tended, as being the least
valuable animals about the clachan. They
may often be seen chasing various quadrupeds
off these raised promenades, the luxuriant green
growth generally to be seen there in the
summer proving a strong temptation to the
stock. Often the outer wall is built of turfs;

and even when of stone, skill in masonry not
being general, a bank is thrown against it as
an additional support. Various explanations
have been attempted of this peculiar Hebridean
mode of erecting huts, such as want of wood
to stretch the roof over the whole so as to form
eaves, a former state of great cold demanding
thick walls, want of constructive knowledge,
and so on. It seems to us natural, that thick
walls should be thus erected by those without
constructive ability, even although they had
the knowledge; and that the houses are built
in the most natural mode to resist severe winds,
which are well known to sweep over this
"ultima Thule" with unrestrained violence.

We thus find the Esquimaux in Greenland
building similar dwellings, doubtless for similar
reasons. They are thus described. "The walls
are all built alike, six feet high and four feet
thick, of stones and turf. There is a roof of
rough timbers and boards; then the whole,
roof and walls, are covered with heavy sods,
which grow green, and convert the hut into
a sort of mound."

A thin unmortared wall could offer no resistance to cold blasts driven with the force of all the furies; and if a young Benedict were to build an eaved dwelling with his limited and imperfect materials, the roof some rough night might take French leave, and go dancing across the hills.

On the top of the thatched dwelling, whence the smoke finds an exit, the colony of fowls belonging to the house finds warmth and a congenial roost. This artificial heat is said to make them lay much more readily than they would otherwise do. It supplies them with a sort of tropical climate at all seasons, for the peat fire is never extinguished, nor allowed to lapse, night or day. At the same time, there is the drawback of having their eggs always impregnated with a subtle flavour of peat-smoke, which to some palates is an insurmountable obstacle to their enjoyment. No wonder the diminutive creatures lay constantly, such fires are kept up beneath. Many put almost a creel of peats, of which eight or nine go to a country cart, on the fire at a time. This is accounted for by the fact that, notwithstanding, or rather in consequence of their walls, the damp keeps the huts cold and comfortless. The rain running off the roofs renders the walls exceedingly damp, although turfs are placed in the hope of its running over them.

Then the floor is the plain earth; one large bench is formed of earth, peat, or stone, and is the family lounge, while occasionally a rude wooden chair is placed for the head of the family. Indeed, the interior comforts are both few and far between; at least, as far as the contracted space will allow them to keep separate.

The live stock, cows, horse, sheep, &c., keep one end of the dwelling; the hens roost nearer the other bipeds, and nothing but a small edging of stones divides the different inhabitants—sometimes not even that.

They say the cows like to have their company and see the fire, and as they are their great mainstay, they pet them accordingly; spoil them with fish-bones for sweetmeats, and treat them with great familiarity generally.

The furniture consists of a large chest or two, and sometimes a half-box bed; very little further, excepting the pots in which every article of food in the Lews is conscientiously boiled, and a few necessary dishes for porridge, fish, and potatoes.

Fifty years ago, there was only one bowl in Carloway district, and that was at Dalebeg, three miles away. It was sent for whenever the minister came over from Lochs—as he did every third Sunday—that they might do honour to their spiritual superior. There was at that time no spoon with which to eat an egg, and indeed such an article is a rarity even now. When the minister asked for a knife, he was told they once had a shoemaker's knife, but they did not know where the highly prized article had gone, it having doubtless been too carefully laid by.

One also hears much here of the bonnet of Dune Carloway, and on inquiry it turns out to have been a celebrated Kilmarnock bonnet— one of those everlasting, indestructible inventions for carrying wool "where the hair ought to grow," now famous alike in song and story. This bonnet belonged to the community, like their moor and their history, and on the rare occasions when any enterprising member wended his solitary way to the great city, he was carefully intrusted with its use for the journey, to sustain the honour and glory of the clachan. How they managed when two were struck with the same idea of proceeding to "the capital" we never could clearly make out.

At that time, we are told, an active maid-servant received only 5s. per annum, out of which she had to repair damage done during her service; while the men-servants were paid from 30s. to 40s., and even from 10s. to 20s. a year. Their wages to-day may be calculated at an average of £3 for maidservants; while men receive from £8 to £10. We have often hired able-bodied men at 7s. 6d. to 9s. per week, which is yet above the average pay of labourers in Irish country districts.

The oldest dress we saw was that of a man in knee-breeches and "hoggars," or footless stockings, which was said to represent the former apparel. But in 1790 Buchanan tells us, " The men wear the short coat, the feilabeg, and the short hose, with bonnets sewed with black ribbons around their rims, and a slit behind with the same ribbon in a knot. Their coats are commonly of tartan, striped with black, red, or some other colour, after a pattern made, upon a stick, of the yarn." He adds, as to the women, " the *arrisats* are quite laid aside —being the most ancient dress used. It consisted of one large piece of flannel that reached down to the shoe, and fastened with clasps below, and the large silver brooch at the breast, while the whole arm was entirely naked. The ladies made use of the finer, while common women used coarser, kinds of flannel, or white woollen cloths." " The *breeid*, or curtah, a fine linen handkerchief fastened about married women's heads, with a flap hanging behind their backs, above the guilechan (or small plaid), is mostly laid aside." To this we may add, that to-day the unmarried women wear their own strong hair in a neat roll, as the only head-dress, coming out in a clean white "mutch" the morning after their wedding, and never after do we see them without this badge of "authority."

One article of the toilet we find in general use in the present day, according to competent female authorities, and that is red ink. The close dark house, oppressed with pungent reek, is by no means favourable to good colour in the cheeks of the young girls, who thus endeavour, by this simple and cheap cosmetic, to rival the belles who "painted with cinnabar."

The first necessity of existence in such a damp climate is fuel, seeing so little aid to comfort is derivable from the dwelling. Consequently a winter store, or indeed a store for the whole year—as the summer is about as destructive to fuel as the winter—is the first desideratum, never to be overlooked. Fortunately for the poor people, it is generally plentiful and at hand. Every cotter is allotted a portion of the adjacent moor, in which to cut peats sufficient to supply his wants. This always accompanies the lot as a necessary adjunct. A cotter will cut enough in a day or two to last him the year through, but peats require to be well dried in the sun, and, as this depends on the summer, most cotters take care to have a good supply in advance, for fear of a wet year. After cutting, they are lifted into ricks, and afterwards accumulated in still larger stacks. From these last they are carried in as required. A stack or two is placed at the side of the cot, the remainder being left on the moor; but, if the winter is severe or prolonged, they have often to carry creel after creel from the moor to the house, often a mile or more distant, in most unpleasant weather.

The peat on the west side is remarkably good—hard, black, and dense, burning with great heat and intensity. That on the east is scarcely so good; but that of the country generally is of a very superior character. The continuous but not ordinarily very heavy rains, and the slight elevations of the hills, seem particularly favourable conditions for its growth. This has been recently calculated to require fifty to a hundred years per foot, which latter figure may be taken as a rough estimate even for the black fibrous peat in some localities. These fibres, or roots of various peat plants, have been observed to communicate with and draw nourishment from the rocky substratum, being thus supplied from the soil direct. On the other hand, the spongy brown peat is more especially a *moss*, drawing its supplies from the air and the moisture. The former, the principal one in this country, is considered by far the slowest of growth; but yet, from its double sources of supply, may not be so languid in its progress here as is generally supposed.

The various Druidical remains have been cleared of peat that had grown over them often to the height of several feet, in one case six. No one can say for certain how long it is since these monuments of our ancestral faith have been allowed to weep unregarded over the peat that hugged their knees; but, if the peat is a tell-tale, the above calculation of a foot a century would give but six centuries since the feet of votaries left unvisited the ancient fane.

Fuel from the moor, meal from their crops, and an occasional fish from the neighbouring sea, supply food and warmth.

With wool from their own sheep, the women make their own and their men-folk's raiment; and ready money is a thing almost unknown in many families, as it is never required, except in a year of scarcity. Yes, it is wanted for one article, tobacco — for all are inveterate smokers of the most atrocious twist.

No visitor can help being struck by the fact that in the Lews there is an intelligent people still living in the most primitive of known dwellings—dwellings that carry us back to the earliest dawn of civilisation—and that men in contact with English cultivation, many of whom have learned to speak and write the English tongue, are more degraded than the Africans in their habitations.

Many of the people of the West are indebted to civilisation for scarcely anything but tobacco, the Government being felt only through the want of stimulating drinks—a want never felt by Highlanders or Islanders in the olden time, so long as the land would raise a crop of barley.

We were much struck with the healthy appearance of the children, who are rarely deformed in any way; and as rarely succeed in concealing their natural proportions. We have seen half-naked urchins running out bare-limbed among the snow, although but the minute before "dusting" themselves, like sparrows, among the warm peat ashes. Yet a common statement among the people is to the effect that the rising generation cannot compare for physical strength and stamina, as well as for immunity from disease, with that now passing or passed away. They account for this by the want of animal food, which was formerly plentiful among them, but is now rarely indulged in; also by the use of tea and sugar, which have replaced the more healthy native beer consumed among them in former days, and even yet occasionally manufactured surreptitiously for home use.

Delicate chests and rheumatic pains, the latter becoming very prevalent in the damp climate, they account for by the absence of their accustomed home-made whisky, to keep out the everlasting wet to which they are subjected. Indeed, it is not unnatural to suppose that their systems are becoming debilitated from the want of a more stimulating diet to resist the constant encroachments of a trying climate, to which, from the nature of their avocations and the condition of their dwellings, they are continually exposed.

Still, it is an unquestionable fact, vouched for by the medical practitioners long settled in the country, that tubercular consumption is never found among natives who have always remained in the Lews. Strangers have not the same certainty of immunity, as they may have carried the seeds of the disease along with them. Natives who have been away for a time, especially girls on service, not seldom return smitten unto death. So it cannot be said to be the native constitution, so much as the conditions of their existence, to which we must look for an explanation. The quantity of fish oil and marine products devoured may have a beneficial influence, but, above and before all, our conviction is that we must look to the healthy effect of the blessed peat-reek, with which, during half their existence, their lungs are impregnated. Whenever they leave the health-giving outer atmosphere, it is to enter into a strongly antiseptic one. And as they are likewise of a stout habit of body, as a rule, they are peculiarly fitted for the exigencies of their life.

To see the buxom girls sitting singing on the wet moor under the moist sky, herding their kine by the day together; or the well-favoured fisherman, as he "sings in his boat on the bay," you understand the advantage of a good suit of fat to supplement their sound woollen raiment.

It is Communion Sunday. Let us stroll up between the black houses, with their background of huge peat stacks, and see the congregation gathering to worship. Strapping, hard-featured men from Ness, stout "buirdly" men from the East or from Uig, gather in groups to the meeting. All the houses in the various clachans have their visitors, making inroads on their stores; all with the slightest claim to relationship are free and welcome. So they stream along, not to the church, but, wet or dry, to the miniature Carnac, spreading out from the pulpit on the moor. What a crowd of blue umbrellas! Every one has a blue umbrella, be it rain or shine. Do you think that fisherlad would sit on the same stone with Mari, if there was no miniature firmament to slip their heads under, and make them fancy they were "all the world" to each other? Would Donald find room for Black Kate on the same boulder, with a little assistance from his arm, if he could not cover his head like an ostrich and fancy he was hidden?—hidden, indeed! See those three cailliachs enjoying the luxury of a board laid on two squares of gneiss, and unlimited scandal, with their heads together— would they dare push their noses under each other's caps, under the eye of the "minister," were it not for the navy blue? "Who has contracted? Will it be a match? Did they meet first at the Uig communion? Will her father

give her a cow? Was he in luck at Fraserburgh? Look at Ann sharing her shawl with
Haramutch! are they not kind?"—"It'll pe
a teer market! The trovers have pot all the
cheep! The factor ses non podies must kill
a cauf!" And what does the minister say,
Murochy Shawbost, thou great "Professor"?

Indeed! have we professors here? what do
they profess? A great deal more than they
can understand, much less teach; for they
profess that widely embracing idea, *Christianity*,
and yet they will——but men were ever the
same, though manners do sometimes prove a
little different.

Are you desirous of transacting business
with any one on the opposite end of the
island?—wait till the communion—there they
all are, you see! Norman the Horse, so called
because he sits in a cart occasionally, and lets
the horse take its time, as he always does
himself; Murdo the Horse, strong as a Clydes-
dale, who fell over a cliff only to spoil the
sea-beach, and relieved the tedium of life
fighting all comers in Hudson's Bay; Donald

Sätan, who drives like Jehu; and there is our own Donald, with a swing and a step like a captain of free lances, and a face that makes your heart jump. Donald Ban, "O fallow fine," how your laugh rings through our head!

THE SEA.

"BLUBBER and oil! they smell terribly!" remarked a sensitive Briton to a local heiress in Hammerfest. "Ah! yes; but the smells is very good for the monies," was the practical reply. So in the Lews—the fish occasionally smell terribly, but are "very good for the monies." Without them, we much question whether this large population would not subside into the peat bog, on the edge of which they sit and bob for the gadidæ. At the same time the bulk of the fishermen are only amateurs, seeing they cannot go to sea in their open boats during a great portion of the year. The severity of the weather thus prevents the skill that constant employment would secure. Perhaps the short days of the long winter, by putting a stop almost entirely to all outdoor labour, greatly tend to foster lazy habits, while the climate seems to exercise a drowsy influence alike on natives and strangers. Those ports to which nature has been least attentive in giving facilities seem to have stirred up the inhabitants to overcome the difficulties of their position, unless we must allow their greater energy to arise more from the difference of race. Thus Ness, the most successful and enterprising district, is peopled by a fine, tall, powerful race of Norwegian origin, while most of the others are inhabited by Celts with a very slight intermixture of northern blood, not sufficient to startle the dreamy Gael into resolute continuous action.

The average season's fishing per boat, about the Butt, is 3,000 ling—many boats reaching 4,coo to 5,000. To these may be added large quantities of cod, and the commoner fishes known to English commerce as "offal." From the Butt down to the West Coast as far as Carloway, the boats in use are such as may be drawn nightly upon the beach, with six men each as a crew.

At Carloway, Uige, and Bernera, where there are secure harbours, the boats are larger, carry a crew of eight men, and are capable of riding through a stiff gale. Such boats full of ballast are too heavy to row, while, being undecked, they have not the advantage of giving the men confidence : indeed, although capital sea boats, they are either too large or too small. The cod and ling fishery commences in November, and continues until July, when the bulk of the fishermen proceed to the east of Scotland herring fishery for two months. Through a foolish rivalry on the part of the curers, the herring fishery in the Minch commences practically in April, although the fish are not fit for curing at that early season, and the only result is the glutting of the markets with a most inferior article that will not keep, and so destroying the character of Lews herring among consumers. It continues more or less until the boats leave for the Wick fishing. Of late the unprecedentedly large takes at Barra withdrew a great many boats from Stornoway, but the last two seasons have been comparative failures there.

Herring may generally be taken in small quantities in the various sea lochs of the Hebrides during the winter : they are then employed as bait for the white fishing. In Stornoway Bay they are used for the hake and haddock fishing, in which an immense quantity of mussels, carted from the west, are also used.

These are important branches of industry in Stornoway. Hakes are cured extensively for the southern markets. Haddocks are numerous, excellent, and of large size, frequently 8 lb. to 10 lb. weight. Latterly they have been salted for export, as they cannot compete with those from the East of Scotland as smoked Findons, from the time required in transit. In the west the haddocks are in request as bait for cod and ling, as are also the conger eels. The skins of the latter being so tough, they are exceedingly difficult to withdraw from the hooks without the robber impaling itself. The most constant supply of bait for the deep-sea white fishery, however, is derived from the halibut and plaice, as they are always to be had if any fish are going. Turbots are not numerous as a rule, although halibuts go by this name among the fishermen, which is apt to confuse a stranger and give him false impressions. The turbot is known as the "quern-shaped flounder," from its circular shape. Skates of many species are numerous and of large size; five feet across the wings is not uncommon, and fifty to a hundred of ordinary dimensions frequently come ashore in one boat. Coal-fish are numerous in some parts, and are cured in the same manner as hake. A market is found for them among the poorer classes in Ireland.

The position of these Hebridean fisheries is as unsatisfactory as can well be imagined, and evidences the utter want of enterprise and self-reliance of the bulk of the inhabitants. Nearly all the boats in the cod and ling, haddock, lobster, and herring fisheries have hitherto belonged exclusively to the curers, although lately the men seem to have bestirred themselves to secure the possession of a few. For the use of the boat the men pay one share, each of the crew having one also. They are also bound to deliver to the curer who owns it all cod and

ling captured, at a stated price, varying from
8*d.* to 1*s.* for each ling, and 4*d.* to 6*d.* for each
cod. Any other fish caught, after sufficient have
been laid aside for bait, are divided amongst
the crew for the use of their families, one cod
per man being allowed them for the same purpose. Formerly the price included everything,
and the fish was delivered whole; but the men
so often brought the fish without the livers, that
the curers agreed to give them the livers and
reduce the price. Gradually, however, the men
sought both the extra price and the livers, and
they came to be theirs by use and wont, the men
agreeing to gut and behead the fish before de-
livering them to the curer's agent. The agent
has thus only to remove the backbone and throw
them into the pickling-tub. The heads the men
divide among themselves, while the garbage is
removed by the women to the land as manure.
Cods are seldom handed to the curers unless
when taken in quantity, the price given
being so much less than for ling. The curer
supplying thus the boat and the gear, the men
are supposed to supply their own long-lines,

costing each from 30s. to £2. But in general these have also to be supplied on credit. Besides, many months have to be got over, during which there is little or no fishing, when the men have to be supplied on credit with meal for themselves and families. For all such credit accounts they are not only charged exorbitantly, but interest is added as well, while the value of the season's take is not supposed to be due until the end of the fishing.

In the meantime, as the value of the several shares is never very great, the chance is that the drawings of the men,—acting as they naturally do with the recklessness of speculators, superadded to the recklessness of those who can have no idea of how they stand,—will be over, rather than under, what they ought to receive. Now the system of the curers is to endeavour to keep them in debt, so that they may be obliged to fish for them the following year, and yet not to allow them so much credit as to be irretrievably involved. The effect of this is exceedingly curious to an onlooker in one of the wholesale stores kept by the several

curers. There, the best salesman is that man
who can sell the least, and not the most, to the
men; who, when a fisherman demands a few
yards of cloth, can send him away believing that
one yard will suffice, or persuades him that his
old oilskins will keep out the storm for another
season. Notwithstanding all this, the curers
have got the most of the men irretrievably in
debt, and it is not unusual for a crew of eight
men to have a standing debt of £100, or more,
in the curer's books. As the curers have no
mutual confidence, but pursue a cut-throat policy
of mutual antagonism, the men find themselves
so much in request that they make no effort to
extricate themselves from their financial difficulties, and when more credit is refused by one
curer, threaten to bind themselves to another
for the next season. Or let one crew be broken
up, and each member considers himself free,
despite his debts, to fish for any other who may
engage him.

In this way the credit system, springing at
first from the poverty of the population, and
aggravated by the mistaken policy of the curers,

has rendered the financial condition of the Hebridean fisheries most unsatisfactory alike to
fishermen and curers, and prejudicial to the
moral and social advancement of the people.
The debts owing by the fishermen are purely
fictitious, probably not 40 per cent. being *bonâ*
fide value received, and not 20 per cent. ever
likely to be realised. The men, knowing they
are greatly overcharged, retaliate by saying,
" But we don't intend to pay ;" and in place
of glorying in the commercial success of those
who have undoubtedly built up an important
industry among them, they hope for nothing
better than their failure, that all standing debts
may be thus written off. Many who have saved
a little money, put it in the bank, in place of
paying off the debts running on at a high
interest ; and it is not uncommon for a crew,
on receiving the balance remaining after a
successful year's fishing, to march off with it to
the bank. This done, they immediately return
and open a fresh account, utterly neglectful of
the fact that for every shilling they may receive
in interest from the bank, they are charged ten

for the credit given. The most direct evidence of the want of enterprise or self-reliance is the rarity of any fisherman or crew—out of Ness— owning their boats. Rather than risk a few pounds in such an enterprise they would keep savings shut up for years, and allow the curer to receive the high rate of interest for money in- vested that one share for the boat generally brings. This, again, may arise from the fact that the Lews boat-builders are the curers them- selves, and they put such a high price upon the boats supplied that the men are unwilling to purchase at the rate charged. There can be no question that, if the boats were owned by the men or their skippers, they would last far longer, as well as prove an additional impetus to work. At present time is of no value—a good day for fishing is allowed to pass by because it is in the middle or end of the week, and to-morrow may be stormy. Or they have no bait for the long lines, or none for the small lines with which to procure it. In one port the only bait they had was limpets; but these had been completely stripped off the rocks by the

constant necessities of old and young, and it
was a hard day's work for a crew to procure
sufficient to bait a set of lines. At a few miles
distant mussels could be readily procured by
the payment of 3*d.* per barrel as blackmail to
the proprietor, and yet they could not muster
sufficient enterprise to run up in their boats for
a supply that would have saved them many a
day's rambling over the rocks when they might
have been at sea. Every other man has an
explanation of and a panacea for this evil spirit
of laziness. Some blame the potatoes, which
have been the curse of Ireland—some blame
the want of security of tenure of their lots,
which they have no interest in improving. If
fishermen are to have lots, let them have
security of tenure, so that they may spend their
odd time and extra money in improving them,
to their own advantage and that of the proprietor. For our own part, we are not satisfied
that a thorough fisherman need have a lot at all
—indeed, we believe that if the fisheries of the
Hebrides were energetically prosecuted the men
would be far better off without land to draw

away their attention from an industry far more lucrative, when properly undertaken, than any petty cultivation. This does not apply, however, to the present state of this industry, when the men cannot possibly support their families without lots.*

The northern fisheries are sufficiently extensive as well as sufficiently various to keep able men at work the whole year through, in place of a few months only, thus increasing their skill and value even for the fisheries already afoot. Why should English boats be fishing on the Hebridean banks when not a boat is afloat from the Hebrides? With suitable boats and the new facilities for forwarding supplies to the great towns, the cry of "nothing to do" would soon be succeeded by "not sufficient men to do

---

* The lots, too, ought distinctly to be leased to the cotters that they may be encouraged to improve them. We are told that at one time the cotters were offered leases with *only* fifty-four rules attached, the transgression of one cancelling the right of the lessee. One old man, at Ness, laughed heartily at the document; sagely remarking that he could not keep ten commandments for a mansion in the sky, much less fifty-four for a black house in the Lews. We much fear, however, that a lease in any case would be practically valueless.

it," as in the South to-day. But, for this, capital must be invested in more suitable vessels, and the men trained to work them, as they are unfit to do so now. This requires time.

The skippers of the Lews boats have not the absolute control thereof, but more the position of chairmen, excepting in the management of the boat at sea, when it is essential to obey the orders of one head. Their only extra perquisites consist of the boat's share of "offal" added to their own, and a stone of wool at the end of the fishing. Each individual member of the crew agrees personally with the curer, and has as much say in the agreement as the nominal man in charge. And what a scene is this same signing of the agreement! In comes a crew, who sit round the room in all sorts of attitudes, from the stern, immovable, unreadable face of the hardy old fisherman, above the hard, immovable figure, to the merry-eyed, restless, half-smiling boy in his first or second season. But all have a keen, bargain-making look, as if they knew the full value of their labour, and valued the *dolce far niente* far too much to sell work under its full value.

Now comes the distant cannonading, the
skirmishing, the advancing musketry, as the
curer tells his tale and states his terms. They
must know everything, you must enter minutely
and confidentially into the state of the markets,
the low war prices and the high prices of everything you have to expend. They question you
keenly and minutely, discuss the probable terms
of opposing curers, and, whatever they may intend to do, take care that you understand they
are not going a-begging, but are independent
merchants bringing their labour to the best
market. Every one has objections which he
states volubly, and every one of which, in
different mouths, has to be answered separately
time after time. They rarely agree the first
time of asking, as it would look too easy a
victory, and the fact that they may be head
over ears in debt to the man before them abates
not a jot their self-sufficiency. So they retire
to reconsider the question, and have a palaver
among themselves. Then they return and
restate the various objections, which a mutual
confabulation has shown to be most important.

These being answered, the agreement is written out, and then comes the tug of war. Who is to sign first? Not the skipper; it would look as if he had a private object in influencing the crew in favour of this particular curer. No; he won't! Now, Thoramutch (Norman), says the curer, with a persuasive smile, like the historical spider to the fly. Thoramutch shakes his head and laughs. Ian! come, now; you'll sign. But Black John vouchsafes not a sign of recognition, nor appears to have heard a sound. Murochy and Georish are alike appealed to in vain. An Englishman would have broken his heart, or two or three heads, by this time; but a Scotch curer lays down his pen with a laugh and a joke. "Why won't they sign?" asks an observant stranger. Who knows? they have no reason; perhaps they wish some more talk just for amusement; perhaps they desire to worry the curer a bit. They don't expect to get any further advantage, but they don't like to be bound, and have not the moral courage to be first to bind themselves to what afterwards may not prove satisfactory.

E

At length a most heartrending appeal to some particular friend among the crew, as the curer pushes the pen towards him, induces him to touch the handle, with a look as if it were red-hot iron, and the curer then takes down his name; two or three more follow, and the matter seems settled. Is it? Ian Dhub sits with the same imperturbable face, as if deaf and dumb, and the most feeling appeals won't even elicit a wink. The pen is again laid down, and after an amount of active and passive resistance, sufficient almost to have stayed the advance of a German army, the list of names is complete, and the last hand, which has hitherto lain in the owner's pocket for fear of being surreptitiously secured, has been induced to touch with the point of its finger the deadly weapon that binds him to fish in No. 10,000 for the season to come. The men rarely sign themselves, although often able to write; touching the pen is considered quite as binding.

FOOD AND CLOTHES.

THE economy, or want of economy, domestic and otherwise, of the inhabitants of this northern desert may well be a source both of interest and instruction. Ways and customs long since banished from the more accessible portions of the empire yet hold their ground in the remoter districts, and the celebrated and still prolific mother of invention brings forth her peculiar offspring.

As you pass along some quiet path, a bevy of strapping damsels with uncovered limbs issues from the rude doorway of a "black house." Those same limbs have been dexterously plied "waulking" a new-made strip of blanketing, or so-called "kilt," as they name the home-made cloth of any or no colour, whether for the trews of the master, or the petticoat or skirt of his dame.

Towards the north-east the spindle and distaff may still be constantly seen at work, but in our immediate neighbourhood the spindle is only used in twisting the thread, the wheel having entirely surperseded the more primitive distaff as a spinner. Formerly the girls, when employed out of doors during the summer, made the warp with the distaff and spindle, as it made a more regular and better warp than the wheel, and could be worked at by fits and starts between other outdoor labours. Then, during the winter, they worked at the weft on the wheel itself, by which to complete the materials for the weaver.

Near the mouth of Loch Carloway is a long cliff, barely out of the perpendicular, which was pointed out to us as having been scaled by a woman, who continued to work her distaff and spindle during the ascent. Although the rocks were very smooth and exceedingly steep, we can almost credit the tale, as we have our-selves seen women carrying crèels of seaware up almost inaccessible cliffs. Of course, they are greatly assisted by the prehensile action of the bare feet—boots being too valuable to be worn among rocks or on the moor.

Place aux dames ; let us first consider in detail the domestic arrangements in the hands of the women, and trace in order the result of their industry, which is untiring, if not always regulated to the best advantage.

As soon as the family is astir in the morning, the grown-up girls, or whoever is entrusted with the duty, prepares to go to the stack of peats on the moor for a supply of fuel. Before setting out with her creel, she partakes of the roasted potatoes which it is the common custom of the country people to place in the ashes of the day's fire before turning in for the night. On her return the fire is made up, and cooking commences, which consists in boiling a huge pot of potatoes, to be eaten with butter or milk by the family ; or perhaps a piece of fish, fresh or salted, should the men be fishermen ; or a few herring, brought over last season from Wick or Fraserburgh. If the potatoes are finished, as they will be in spring, porridge takes their place, this breakfast being eaten about ten or eleven in winter. These dishes form the principal part of their diet, to which may be added, when the family is well off, eggs from their poultry, together with the universal, wholesome, and palatable barley bread, and of late years an occasional cup of tea. A repetition of this meal again about six in the evening may be said to constitute the customary diet.

It may be here observed that, as the white oats does not grow well in most parts of the Lews, the old native black oats is still cultivated; it has a much smaller grain and smaller yield generally, and is too dark for porridge. This, then, they principally consume in the form of sowens, made thus—As the meal comes from the mill it is steeped in water, until the grain dissolves and the whole sours : this takes from three days to a week. The mixture is then strained, and the fine allowed to settle, while water is added regularly to keep it to a right consistence. This is kept for making a kind of pudding called sowens, which, when well strained and not allowed to become too sour, is a most agreeable and exceedingly nourishing food. Eaten with milk, it is a favourite supper both among the natives of the Hebrides and many parts of the mainland of Scotland. Occasionally they slaughter one of their small sheep or some of their chickens, and therewith make soup, adding a few cabbages from their gardens. "Gardens" is certainly a dignified title for the small patches of land surrounded with high dykes, containing a few scared-looking cabbages, and overtopped by an interior circle of lank willow wands destined for the ribs of creels. Excepting pots for boiling, which is an Hebridean's only mode of cooking, a gridiron for firing the cakes of oatmeal or barley is the sole utensil. It is set on two long hind legs and two short fore ones —like a kangaroo—and thus suited to the fire on the floor. Potatoes, now so universal, have only been introduced about a century, and tea has not been at all used in the West more than twenty years. A field at Dalbeg is known as the "tea field," from having been once manured by the tea thrown ashore from a wreck, no other use being found for it. Before the notorious root brought life or laziness to the now numerous population, the inhabitants were necessarily scant and red deer numerous. Venison, game, fish, milk, and the produce of the land they chose to cultivate, and the cattle or sheep they could afford to keep, enabled them to keep the wolf from the door. At present they are of necessity omnivorous; no fish comes amiss to them. Skate kept for such a length of time that when raised to the mouth it attacks the nostrils like a bottle of smelling salts, and known and beloved as sour skate, is a favourite with all. Indeed, it often exercises after a time a fascinating influence over the originally contemptuous Sassenach.

What is the reason for this? Is it not merely another form of necessity for something tasty and stimulating to the palate, to relieve the monotony of porridge or potatoes?

Dog fish (*Spinax*) kept for a short time and half dried, like the skate without salt, is by some considered a tit-bit, by others of more delicate stomach eaten for lack of something

more tasty. Perhaps desire for revenge for the
ravages committed on the ling, and to utilise
the myriads of these savages dragged perforce
into their boats, may influence some. The belly
should not be eaten by any unaccustomed
palate, nor allowed to enter any ordinary
stomach—it is so rank and oily. The back,
however, when kept a short time and properly
prepared, we found not uneatable. All sea-fowl
they eat with avidity, the cormorant being
eagerly sought for. In some parts the Solan
goose, fearfully offensive and rank though it be,
is eaten when young, fat, and tender, like
"little Billee." Even some species of gulls, by
the enterprising, are found to be eatable when
skinned. Almost every kind of shell-fish is
willingly received, and limpets are eaten in
great quantities by the poor when they run out
of better food. They are understood to be very
strong and sustaining food, but the intestine,
which they declare to be injurious, is always
drawn out before eating. Cockles boiled in
milk, cockle soup, pickled cockles, are all held
by connoisseurs to be super-excellent when well

managed. Sufficient may be had in Stornoway
for a few halfpence to form a most delicious
repast. Scallops are always heartily welcome,
and, besides their edible properties, the shells
are in general use—the convex as a butter-
scoop, the flat being delegated to the milk-
basin as a creamer.

The sea, the sea, the generous sea, has not
yet done its best for the native gastronomy.
Sea birds, sea fish, shell-fish—these are not all.
Besides dulse, so well known on the mainland,
they peel and eat the fresh stalks of the
tangle. It tasted to us like a hard turnip,
but is much liked among them, and is doubtless beneficial medicinally as an adjunct to their
diet. Then there is a dark ware called here
" Slochgan" (*Nitophyllum punctatum* ?) that they
boil with butter, and which meets with appro-
bation even among civilised diners. These
latter, however, are more partial to caragoon,
found in quantity on some parts of the coast,
and in common use among the educated inhabitants as a pudding. This ware—the Irish
moss of commerce—when gathered, is carefully

washed, and then bleached for some days in the sun and rain until perfectly white, when it is dried for use. The dried plants when carefully picked so as to be free of impurity, are boiled with milk, and form a pleasant and well-known dish.

Strange to say, although mushrooms are very numerous in some districts, the natives will not eat them. Faery rings are likewise common in the "macher" * near Broad Bay, and the most plausible explanation we have heard of them is, that they spring up like other fungi on the outer circumference of cattle-droppings of old standing, which have been washed out by the rain in regular circles. When they are found on sloping ground they depart from the circular and assume the elongated form in which the manure would run on the slope. The observant salmon-fisher, to whom we owe this explanation, has entirely divested it of all romance.

We have so far considered a few of the "internal" comforts, and will now examine the

* The bent-grown, sandy tracts by the sea.

outward adornment of a Lews inhabitant. From the fact that every cotter owns a few sheep, wool is naturally the first and most important article in use. This is often torn from the animal, Shetland fashion, in place of being clipped. More wretched-looking creatures than these poor little sheep, hanging in rags, cannot be conceived; and one wonders if it is a source of satisfaction to the cotter children to see something more hopelessly ragged than themselves sharing the bleak moor with them. The natural grey wool from the grey sheep is much sought after, as it makes the best stockings without requiring to be dyed. It is also considered to be much softer and warmer than the coloured wools. The wool thus torn or shorn from the sheep gives employment to the family in the winter time, in preparing it for use, and making it up into various garments. Enter a dwelling about this time and you are sure to see it undergoing some manipulation. Here an old woman is carding, there a more vigorous damsel is singing at the wheel. Perhaps a whole side of the room is

occupied by an extensive framework of so
many ells, about which the yarn is coiled into
hanks from the reels; or a smaller framework,
like a double triangle, is held in the left hand,
and the yarn twined thereon with peculiar and
great celerity. The wool is manipulated with
the black oil from fish livers, so as to work more
readily, and when spun into thread is ready
for the further process of dyeing. At the
present day, when the thrifty indigo blue is in
great demand, both for the jacket and trousers
of the fishermen and the strong outer petticoat
of the women, other dyes are not so much
employed. The extensive knowledge of native
colours formerly possessed is thus by no means
so common, while at the same time the people
are showing an inclination to purchase a few
pounds of colour from the shops in town, to
save the little trouble necessary to procure the,
in general, much better and more lasting native
article.

Amongst the dyes still in use is the grey
moss called "crotul," which covers the surface
of the outcropping rocks throughout the

country. It yields a fine, rich brown dye,
much used for stockings and other such articles,
seeing it is so easily obtained and always at
hand. Soot, more especially that scraped from
the iron pot suspender, gives a capital maroon
colour, and the wives of those farmers who
still indulge in home-made clothes often make
a good lasting mixture of these two colours.
A first-rate black is extracted from the root
of the water lily, with which plant many of the
small lochs are overgrown; heather, that rare
plant becoming in the Lews, yields a good
yellow; goatsbeard, a green; the root of a
small yellow plant growing in the "macher,"
a fawn colour. It is called *rue*, and is said
to be a species of madder. The root of a
small yellow species of cinquefoil or potentilla,
abundant all over the country, was formerly
generally employed in barking nets and lines,
and is also in use as a yellow dye. It is said to
be superior to cutch, but the latter has almost
entirely superseded it.

Thus any cotter is really independent of
civilisation for his clothes, the wool coming

from his own sheep, spun by the women of his house; dyes are good, and easily procured; and the yarn is woven into cloth by his neighbour or himself. Besides the common mordant, they use "sooriks" (wood sorrel) with blue and black; alum with yellow; while common salt and sea water are sufficient for others. Dulse is also used to give a fine purple colour to blue, and otherwise improve it and make it clearer. You often see newly made clothes of capital quality held together by wooden skewers or nails in place of buttons; and, as nearly all are independent of boots or shoes, and many men as well as women never wear them except on Sundays, there are families that scarcely require to enter a shop from year's end to year's end. A shop! Beg pardon! there are none in the country; all are merchants. And why use boots, where your first step outside the door takes you to the knees in mud and filth, and your first step inside sends you as deep in manure?

The light of the fire is in most cases the only one that irradiates the hut of the Lewsman, but when occupied by a fisherman's family the iron lamp may be found hung from the thatched roof or some projecting beam, filled with fish-liver oil, the wick formed of twisted rag or the pith of rushes.

But before we leave the family blinking round the peat fire, telling interminable tales, or "crooning" never-ending songs, we will introduce the reader to a favourite *bonne bouche*. Take two eggs, with a little butter and meal, whip them all well up together, and place on the top of a hot barley bannock. Spread evenly over, and hold a live peat above until it firms sufficiently to allow the cake to be toasted before the fire. This done properly, no instructions are required as to its disposal. It is a favourite "piece" for herd-boys; and one was formerly due to whoever discovered a cow after calving—one or two eggs being given according to the sex of the calf. With beef at a premium and cattle at a ransom, we advise, in the interests of society and the herd-boys, an immediate return to the practice.

FARMING AND FISHING.

STEPPING out of doors for a time, we shall
examine into their mode of working their
lots, or allotments, which in general stretch
in narrow patches parallel to each other, and
outward from the row of dwellings constituting
the customary clachan. A few small stones
erected at intervals form the only divisions;
so that in the autumn, when the crop is housed
and the potatoes pitted, one common stretch
of barren-looking land, over which the cattle
and sheep roam at will, surrounds the various
villages. Dotted over this are the circular
walled gardens, to prevent the ingress of half-
starved stock, and resembling the mouths of
Eastern wells sprinkled over a desert. About
the beginning of spring every man who goes

F

to Stornoway re-appears with a new spade over his shoulder, to replace that worn out during the last season; their spades being only made to last one season. Immediately the beings who have been half dormant during the winter may be seen hard at work in the fields until the ground that has been untouched since harvest has been all turned up and is ready to receive the barley, oats, or potatoes reserved as seed. The whole family is employed at this time, and few crews can make up their complement of men " until the potatoes are in."

The vast mass of putrescent matter formed by the litter and bedding of cattle, sheep, or horses during the whole winter, is carried out to the fields in creels, thus turning up a malarious hotbed in the very heart of their dwellings.

The roof is next taken off, and likewise borne in creels to the land. Everything betokens unnatural activity, but, notwithstanding pure air and plenty of work, how they manage to escape pestilence is not apparent to the uninitiated. The roofs are thatched with the barley. This crop is always drawn up by the roots; the heads are then cut off, and the roots and straw used to thatch the dwellings. When removed, after having been thoroughly impregnated by the soot from the heavy winter fires and half rotted with the winter rains, it is spread on the surface of the potato ground as the most favourable manure for producing a dry root crop. It is only employed as a top-dressing when rain is expected, and is a great difficulty in the way of improving their dwellings, seeing they value this manure at from fifty shillings to three pounds per roof, and consequently look upon tile or slate innovations as robbing them of their potato crop, which is their main subsistence.

During the winter, after every stormy night, the women may be seen at early dawn climbing the steep cliffs from the shore, with heavy creels of seaware on their backs, or rather their hips, for there the weight chiefly rests. This they place in some corner of the lot, and cover over to form a compost along with any fish garbage that may be procurable from the boats. This seaware is seldom used for potatoes, as it is too wet, but is principally employed on the barley ground. When the barley ground is turned up the manure from the stock is simply spread over it, the seed being sown on it, and then harrowed. The rotation crops are potatoes with soot manure, barley with seaware and litter, and oats without any dressing whatever.

No sooner is the hard work of seed-time over than their play-hour supervenes, the time looked forward to by all as the " merriest time of all the glad new year," when the whole household may be seen with a few staves wherewith to erect a roof to their shieling, a creel or two of peats, and a few utensils, driving their cattle and sheep to the distant moor. Here they have erected small dome-shaped dwellings, about six feet in diameter. They are formed of low stone walls, with a turf roof on a framework of sticks, and two opposing doors, where you have almost to creep in order to enter, resembling nothing so much as Esquimaux snow huts. One of these doors is turfed up when the wind blows in that direction; and as soon as it changes to the other side the turfs are taken down, and the other doorway filled up. In the thick walls are openings in which the milk-dishes are placed, and sometimes also an opening next the floor for the head of a sleeper, the feet of any ordinary-sized mortal reaching the opposing wall.

In these primitive hovels do the girls of the family spend six weeks or two months gipsying during June and July. The men take every opportunity to go courting them, as their sweethearts on those occasions always deluge them with the richest of milk and sweetest of butter. It is almost impossible to get girls to go to service at this time, seeing it is looked forward to as *par excellence* the " courting-time." No inducement will entice them to forego this long period of free picnicing amid the heather. The coolness with which a strapping youth will excuse his yawning laziness during his forenoon's work, by stating that he had been away on the moor courting the night before, is most amusing.

The quantity of milk the little Highland cattle will give, when thus feeding on the fresh sweet grass of the distant moors, is very great, and of the richest quality. A large portion is soured or thickened, and carried home across the moor to the rest of the family, while a portion of the butter is salted for winter use. We may say none of it is sold, as the little that is not consumed, or given in kindness to some neighbour who has no lot, is carefully laid by.

But, Credat Judæus! how they do tuck in, and what a change comes o'er the spirit of their dream during those two months. See them step along, light and active, as they set out on their picnic, and you would scarcely believe it was the same party returning, rolling in fat, contributed as rent by the four-legged tenants for their winter lodgings.

Hark! there is great stir and bustle about the port, long ere the picnic time is over. What is it all about? They are pulling up their cod and ling boats for the season, preparatory to setting out for Wick. There is all the wild excitement and shouting inseparable from any general activity among the nervous Celts, lasting for some days. Then the men are scarcely to be seen for a day or two, as they overhaul their clothes and prepare their kits; their little canvas bags are carted over to the steamer, and the place is desolate of its defenders for a time. Only a few old men and young boys are left; and, indeed, no one will remain who can raise a few shillings to pay his passage, and has the necessary strength for the labour at sea. The following lines convey a just idea of the importance attached to this annual trip among the young men and maidens :—

As the sun went down, with golden crown,
   O'er Bernera's rocky ridges,
And threw his rays o'er bights and bays,
   Like fancy fairy bridges,

A maiden sat, without her hat,
   All in the evening breezes
Upon the hills, despising chills,
   And not afraid of sneezes.

"How now ? my dear, what dost thou here ?
   Have quarrelled with your vain beau ? "
"No lover I; while in the sky
   Miss Cloud has got a rain beau."

" Just wait a bit, my little chit "—
   I chucked her 'neath the chin—
" 'Tis kiss and go with a fancy beau;
   Miss Cloud is taken in."

Just as I feared, he disappeared
   Like robber down a skylight,
And poor Miss Cloud wept not aloud,
   But faded in the twilight.

" But who is this, my blushing Miss,
   Comes swinging with his stick ? "
" That's only Jim ; I don't count him—
   He hasn't been to Wick."

" This skipper here, my naughty dear,
   Looks sweeter than he ought."
" Why, don't you see he's nobody ?
   He hasn't got a lot."

I turned aside with humbled pride—
   My heart was very sick ;
No lot I had, and, twice as bad,
   I hadn't been to Wick !

The usual mode of engaging at Wick is for a definite wage, along with board and lodgings. After paying their passage to and fro, and expenses until an engagement is secured, the men can generally return with two or three pounds or more, according to their skill and experience. Down the East coast, on the other hand, the principle is for the men to pay their own board and lodgings, and take the chance of the fishing, being paid so much per cran. This is the mode of arrangement at Fraserburgh, and to this place a better class of men go—men who

are able to pay their way and remain out of
their money until the end of the fishing. If the
fishing is good, they often return from their trip
to this place with £20 to £30—a very large
sum for a Lews man, and sufficient to support
his family in comfort for the remainder of the
year.

After six or seven weeks in Caithness, the
men return home about the end of the first week
in September, improved physically and finan-
cially. Thenceforward for some time they are
very idle—a few boats, perhaps, prosecuting the
lobster-fishing on the west. Fishing for lythe
and saithe, the young of the pollack and coal-fish,
is now looked forward to as the evening employment of the younger members who can manage
to procure a seat in a boat. The former fish
is very numerous along this rocky coast, and,
although soft in the flesh, is a welcome addition to the Lews diet at this season. Besides
the usual white fly, the most killing bait used
here for this species is a hook busked with a
piece of the tail of the dog-fish; in ordinary
weather it is most destructive. The proper

mode of fishing lythe in the loch is to row a
boat slowly with flies attached to strong rods
dragging behind the boat, the ends sunk a foot
or two under water. The boat must be kept
close to the rocks, and the best time for capture
is in the evening, when it is half-tide and rising,
at which periods they may often be captured as
fast as the rod can be drawn in, the two or three
hooks each occupied by a fish from six inches to
a foot or two in length.

About this time the harvest operations are
carried on mostly by the women, as in seed-
time. The potatoes are dug up and creeled
home to be pitted near the houses; the oats
are cut down with the sickle, and the barley
drawn up by the roots. Many hands make
light work as well as quick work; and as the
climate is so variable and untrustworthy, they
never halt in favourable weather until the
grain is all housed. The whole household
is engaged in this work, the children being
withdrawn from school both at seed-time and
harvest.

Nowhere more than in the Lews is the compulsory clause of the Education Bill demanded, as the work of the children is merely nominal in most cases, and could well be dispensed with, to their advantage. During the autumn and winter the grain is prepared at leisure, as the potatoes are first consumed, or nearly so, before the meal is much run upon. When in urgent need of meal, the grain is sometimes dried in an iron pot on the fire, and then taken to the quern or handmill, where, however, a great quantity is necessarily lost, from the difficulty of collecting it as it issues from between the stones. This meal is called "gratanach," is much liked by some people who could not well digest the common meal, and is the ancient way of preparing it. In old times, also, the barley heads were taken, and the grain "switched" out of them, as is done occasionally in some parts even now, and kiln-dried in the husks. To-day, however, the most usual way is by the flail, when the grain is winnowed in the breeze that is always ready for it, and then taken to the kiln. Every six or eight cotters join together and build one of these little huts

for their mutual benefit. A hole is dug in the
centre, with a trench leading to it. This is
covered over so as to support a quantity of
straw, on which the grain is laid. The heat
from a peat fire is led under the straw along
the trench, and the grain thus dried. After
this the grain is taken to one of the little mills,
also erected by the joint efforts of a portion of
the cotters.

Follow one of the narrow mill-lades from
some stream, and you arrive at a little Esqui-
maux-looking hut. Crawl into this, and you
find two good granite stones; suspended over
the centre is a stout bag of woven rushes;
through one corner of this the grain trickles
into a wooden shoe. As the stone revolves, a
projecting stick strikes this shoe and tilts the
contents into the hole in the stone, the shoe
being refilled by the next revolution. The
grain is deposited in a hole in the stonework
on which the millstones rest, the hut itself being
in most cases built of turf. The stones are cut
with great labour and patience out of the granite
rock by the village mason or blacksmith; and

a granite cliff near Dalebeg, on the road from Carloway to Barvas, is often occupied at the base by an industrious millstone hewer. Here and there modern mills have been erected by the proprietor, and let to tenants; all the cotters within a certain district are obliged to send their grain thither, or pay the miller the same as if they did. This is rather a high-handed mode of introducing civilisation. For instance, the people of Uige have to forward their grain to Callanish Mill, either going upwards of twenty miles by road or crossing Loch Roag by boat, when, on arrival, the mill may be full of work, or the weather too stormy to return. Such eventualities often occur. In this way several days are always, and many days often, spent away from home, while the families are awaiting the meal they might have had ground at their doors. A great many people prefer paying the penalty and grinding at their own little mills, and all complain of the great tax thus imposed upon them to enable the worthy miller to pay his rent. The meal once ground, they have provided themselves with sieves through which to take off the rough. These are made of sheepskins, stretched over strong wooden hoops until they are tight as a drum; the perforations are made with a small awl made of a straightened cod-hook with the barb chipped off: this is stuck in a handle of tangle stem, which enables the hand to grasp it readily when heated in the fire. These simple and useful little instruments are in universal use in the Lews for this and similar purposes.

A WEDDING IN THE WEST.

"KATRINA has contracted with Callum Callum," said our friend Norman, the morning after this important preliminary ceremony to the marriage of the couple had been gone through. "They are going into town on Wednesday," he added, this being, of course, to buy the braws and the whisky, preparatory to the great event, which was expected to come off in a fortnight. In the Lews there is always this "contract" previous to marriage. To this a few friends of both parties are invited, when they pledge their troth to each other. As one lad described it, "They sit looking at one another and laughing, and the friends look at them and they laugh, and when all are tired sitting and laughing the friends make them take hands before them all, and promise to be man and wife." Then the spirit of unrest, till then corked in a whisky bottle, is let loose. The select coterie of friends now drink to the health of the pair, and agree as to the extent of their liberality to them; after which, outsiders are allowed to enter, and help to pass the evening merrily. Thus, often these contract parties wind up by singing and dancing through the evening. Immediately thereafter a visit is made to Stornoway by the pair, on foot—or, if fortunate, in a cart—from whence they return gaily bedizened for the sacrifice. The day is now fixed to suit the minister, who is always the autocrat of the district, and may refuse to marry them on account of some trifling crotchet. If they happen to be in luck, however, they may return "one flesh" after a walk of twenty-five miles. This the younger members of the marriage party undertake, walking couple by couple after the bride and bridegroom, neatly dressed and stoutly shod, for the winter season, when marriages are mostly perpetrated, rarely vouchsafes a dry journey. On their return from the religious ceremony they proceed to the house of the bride's parents, where a large party of friends are assembled, ready and anxious to begin the dancing.

It is the month of December in the Hebrides, with its miserably short days and its long evenings by the peat fire. We have shouldered our guns about two hours after nightfall, and are now seeking our uncertain way " o'er muir and mire" to the hut at present occupied by a happy party. Scrambling and tumbling along over awkward stones, soaking "lazybeds," unexpected ditches, and moss holes to be expected and avoided, we at length fancy ourselves near the spot. We fire off our guns as both a notice and an honour, and are soon rushed upon by some wild dancers in their shirt-sleeves, carrying blazing peats to direct our steps. This precaution is rendered far more necessary by our approach to the clachan, where a biped and quadruped host always combine to trample the neighbourhood into a quagmire. The wild figures with their peat torches, directing us, by winding ways, through layers of filth, to the

door of a low miserable-looking dwelling,
resembling the erections in an Arab "tribu,"
would almost lead one to anticipate an encamp-
ment of more than half-naked savages. Stoop
well as you enter the door, and tread warily
up the bed of accumulated manure, several feet
thick, that marks the portion of the dwelling
assigned to the quadrupeds. Hullo friend!
you are bumping against a cow; a quick step
aside, and you are trampling on a recumbent
calf; a half turn in the dim light, and you
narrowly escape going headlong over a placid
old ewe; while your awkward route up the long
room sets all the hens cackling and the cocks
crowing at the plunges of the clumsy Sassenach.

Emerging from the "midden" on to the
earthen floor, you find a fire blazing in the
centre, a few rude chairs around, and a quiet
corner beyond between two beds. The hook
pendant by an iron chain from the roof supports
a potato pot; cakes of oats and barley-meal rest
against gridirons around the fire, about which
the matrons come and go on their domestic
errands. Between the beds a deal table is set

with a little mutton, fowls, and potatoes, not forgetting the whisky bottle, from which to drink the health of the couple—always freely offered to a stranger, and taken neat.

The meal over, a narrow doorway leads into the barn, which has been cleared for the dancing, with the exception of a large pile of straw at one end. The uneven earthen floor has been carefully swept, and spread with a little sawdust, while long boards, set on meal-bags and herring-barrels, extend round the apartment, and already are decorated with stout hearty men and buxom blooming lasses, all ready for action. Savages, indeed! they meet the stranger with the well-bred ease of men and women of the world; no clownish shamefacedness among these quick-witted Celts; no awkward attempts to excuse their primitive hospitality. With that quiet self-contained readiness which is the outward exponent of inbred manliness, they meet your grasp and find you a seat.

Meantime those seated join hands all round, and beat time to the wild Gaelic air sung by two of the girls, all joining in the chorus.

These songs come in as interludes to the dancing every now and then, and may be carried on *ad infinitum*, the number of verses being apparently as unlimited as the powers of memory of the musicians. Many of the girls are also endowed with a facility of improvising extra verses referring to those present, the chorus giving time for composition. The effect of these wild airs filling the rude barn, from the thatched roof of which depend one or two rude lamps, is strange and picturesque. All beat time with great energy, and vie with each other in fluency of utterance. Some restless youngsters now propose a dance, and forthwith two couples are on the floor, dancing to their partners and swinging round, more in the fashion of an Irish jig, dashed with the Reel of Houlachan, than any other known performance. The girls in this take in general the initiative, and, as might be expected when they do all the hard work, show far more energy, enterprise, and endurance than the miserable male creatures who occasionally do a little fishing, to enable them to eke out the

potatoes planted and harvested by their wives
or sisters! The only music to which they dance
is the human voice. A strathspey or other
air is sung in capital time and in thrilling
unison by two or three girls, to whom constant practice in the long winters around
the fire, or on the lonely moor attending the
kine, has given super-excellent and untiring
lungs. Hour after hour, with slight intervals,
will the same girls continue to give tune after
tune, until you begin to fancy them musical
boxes. The airs get mixed up with your ideas
interminably, refusing to leave your aching
brain, from chamber to chamber of which they
re-echo for weeks. Wonderful to relate, with
an occasional but rare glass of whisky, this
cheerful, happy, pleasure - loving race, little
accustomed to variety or severity of excitement,
continue to sing and dance the same half-reel,
half-jig, until three or four in the morning,
when the girls are called off to the bedding
of the bride in another apartment. This ancient
ceremony completed, the men, headed by the
"best" man, proceed to the same room and

undress the bridegroom, placing him in bed also. From this position he hands a glass of whisky to each of the friends who have been admitted thus far, to drink longevity and fertility. They then return to the dancing-room, where they trip it till daylight. Some few may then go home for an hour or two to rest until mid-day, when they awaken the bride, this being the completion of the time-honoured " bedding ceremony" begun on the previous night. The wedding breakfast is then partaken of, and dancing recommences, if it has ever been really stopped; for it is a universal custom for the wearied dancer to throw himself down *with his partner* on the adjacent bed, awakening after a short nap, refreshed and invigorated for another spell, leaving the bed for another couple, for it is seldom unoccupied during the whole time of the wedding. During the afternoon of this, the second day, it is customary for the bridal party, headed, as usual, by the married couple, to set out for a walk of half-an-hour or so, returning to the close and superheated dwellings with a few mouthfuls of fresh air.

The party have now transferred themselves to the dwelling of the bridegroom's father, and here we are once more assembled. As no . barn has been cleared out, we are seated round the blazing fire, and dancing still vigorously on the "house" side of it, the other being occupied principally by the live stock. The peat-reek is pungent, the fire terribly hot, the floor uneven, and the atmosphere close; but the people are determined to enjoy themselves, and we enter heartily into their mirth, dancing through the whole circle of strathspey and reel steps until the assembled eyes are heavy, the feet weary, and the feelings unable to respond to the continued merriment. Ha! there is a fresh face! You must get a partner at once and get up! But the new comer continues stubborn, until a hearty little singer and dancer from the neighbouring village approaches us once more. He is greeted with "Here comes Tolsta," and under his nickname of "Aulach," or "the strong man," is called upon to drag up the new comer, but in vain. We then endeavour to incite the emulation of the various

villages, and start "Garnin," the strong and
tireless, once again. An active partner and
rattling singers from the same clachan soon
infuse fresh spirit, and for another hour
Garnin jumps against Kiriwig, Carloway against
Boroston, and Tolsta against Knock. At
length, the tired performers turn upon the
guest, and insist that he should still again
represent the Dunan, of which he is the only
inhabitant. Choosing a sprightly partner for
a farewell strathspey, the stranger rises, and
for twenty minutes the mischievous lasses ring
out the Highland Fling at racing speed, until
singers and dancers are alike exhausted. As
he turns to his seat, he observes the mother of
the bride, still fresh and handsome, just entering.
Willing to make a last effort to please, he
takes her hand and returns to the floor. Alas!
for appearances: the buxom dame dances with
the foot of fifteen, fresh voices shake a wild
strathspey through the curling smoke, and
the stranger in his distress anathematizes alike
his gallantry and good - nature. At last, thank
heaven! he is leading her to a seat, when a

shout comes of "Here is another!" "You must dance with this one too," and a bright-eyed dame, still stouter than the last, gives promise of still greater activity and endurance. She fulfils it too; and with shaking knees and bumping heart the stranger makes his adieux and stumbles out through the kine, hurrying off to dream of interminable rows of matrons of gradually increasing size and weight, whom he has to whirl round in an endless dance. And where do the others go? Well! truth is strange, and the truth is that, in this year of our Lord, the "bundling" system is still universal in the Lews, and most of the dancers take home their partners and court them in bed until morning!

In this place, we shall say a few words respecting this strange custom, which is too important and universal a habit among the people of the West to be passed over in silence or with a shrug. An intimate acquaintance with the people among whom we were so-journing enables us to assert that most of the unmarried young men pass the winter nights with their sweethearts. The want of light in most dwellings, the numbers of dark corners even in daylight, and the general habit among the people of throwing themselves down on the straw, simply divested of their outer garment, gives every facility for courtship in the Hebridean fashion. As the girls are, at the same time, "very kind," court assiduously, and are possessed of far greater energy than the men, they acquire a great hold on their affections, and seriously influence those youths who might otherwise have enterprise enough to emigrate to the colonies and attempt to better their condition.

Sincerely deprecating the wrath of any Island fair one, we assert that the girls not only work hard to support a husband when captured, but labour assiduously to obtain him. Not only in household matters, but in the labours of the field they never spare themselves, and may often be seen wielding the spade with energy, when the lazy worse-half does nothing but fill and empty his everlasting pipe. Surely nowhere more than in the Hebrides does Ruskin's statement hold good, that smoking is only a wretched excuse for idleness, enabling a man to do nothing without being ashamed of himself.

Thus courting and working, affectionate and good-tempered, never reproaching their lounging mates for idleness, but thankful when they exert themselves to procure a few fish, which the women willingly creel home, the Lews women do everything that women can to render their homes happy, and, let us add, are generally successful. Rarely does one hear of unfaithful wife or cruel husband : nay, we verily believe that a happier class of people, a people thinking less of to-morrow and enjoying themselves more to-day, does not exist. Illegitimacy in the country is so rare as to be merely nominal, while most married couples are eminently fruitful: the children are fat, intelligent, and frolicsome ; the men stout, hearty, and keen-witted ; their active good dames crowning a social edifice of health, peace, and contentment, though it be of the humblest.

Considering all this, one turns away from

the marriage-party of a Lews cotter without
any unpleasant forebodings as to their future,
concluding that if their "lot" is good, their
lot is happy; and as we look round among
the men and maids and consider their ways,
we thank Providence that women may be fond
and men affectionate to an extent of mutual
confidence long expelled from the more civilised
regions of the earth.

A FUNERAL IN THE WEST.

THERE has been a funeral in the village. "The best and truest man inside the road" has passed away, probably from want of medical advice, against which he was bigotedly prejudiced; nor would he taste medicine that had come from a doctor. "They can give you stuff that will kill you in a moment," he said, and put no trust in the Faculty. This part of the coast has the credit of being very healthy, and very seldom is the attentive physician resident at Stornoway called over to Carloway on business. The neighbouring populous clachan of Garnin has only been twice visited by the doctor in forty years—a visit made during our stay being the first in twenty years.

But to the funeral. Down the hill in solemn

procession comes the party, all showing true grief and impressive sobriety of manner.

The coffin, of common deal, stained black, is fastened upon two old oars, and one of the large open fishing-boats swings on the beach, ready to receive the remains of him who has set his last long line amidst the Western waves, heard the keel grate for the last time on the pebbly shore. About forty friends, all stout fishermen, have met to convey the remains of their companion to his last home by the sounding sea, on the island of Little Bernera, where the fishermen of the West all hope to rest. The sail once set, a smart breeze carries us across the Sound to the little sandy creek in close proximity to the graveyard of the island. As there is no proper landing-place, some of the men spring out on the rocks bordering the sandy beach, and hold the boat steady with ropes, while the remainder clamber ashore, and accompany the coffin up the rocky knolls to the cemetery. This is merely a little sandy patch closely packed with mounds, only two or three possessing a stone with the names of the occupants. Here a

consultation takes place as to the proper place
of burial; and this agreed upon, spades are
produced, and the friends around soon excavate
a grave a few feet deep in the sand. The bitter
November blast, that had often borne the dead
to his labours on the deep, now shrieks the
only requiem over his grave, and hurls the
driving sleet in the faces of the mourners. A
passionate burst of heartfelt grief breaks from
the sons of the deceased as they lower the
coffin to its place on the edge of the cliff over
the sea. The grave is then filled up, the friends
bear turfs from the neighbourhood and neatly
cover the mound, a rude stone is placed at the
head and foot, and we thoughtfully wander back
from the little island cemetery, where the winds
and the waves keep watch and ward over so
many "toilers of the sea."

No one has any distinct charge over the
cemetery, but certain scarcely definable portions
of the ground are understood to appertain to
certain families. The deep feeling with which
the fishermen pointed out some rugged mound
as that over a beloved relative, showed how

strongly affectionate was their Celtic nature;
and yet there is not a cemetery in the Lews
worthy of the name, in which the slightest
care is bestowed on the graves after inter-
ment. The enclosure of rude stones here is
very small, the sea having curtailed it, while
it threatens still further to reduce it within a
short period.

On our way back to the boat we halted under
the shelter of a rock, and were supplied by
the friends with a glass of whisky and piece
of biscuit, as the wind was strong, bitterly cold,
and opposed to our rapid return.

No clergyman whatever was present, and no
ceremony took place, nor is it customary, so
far as we understand. It is usual, however, to
have prayer over the coffin, in presence of the
female mourners, before leaving the house.

The boat is again drawn close up to the
slippery seaweed-grown rocks, and the party
re-embark. They sit shivering with their
heads drawn into their jackets, and pipes, lit
under every disadvantage, in their teeth. Now
and again they rouse themselves to shift the

heavy sail as we tack the boat on our zigzag way across the Sound. Everything was conducted with propriety and sobriety, Highlanders always displaying true good feeling on such occasions; and as we jumped half-frozen on to the beach once more, we felt pleased to have joined in the last mark of respect to the kindly face that so often, creel on shoulder, had passed our door.

LOBSTER-FISHING.

IN certain rocky districts this is generally a most remunerative fishing to the Hebrideans. It is prosecuted in stout boats of 15 or 16 feet keel, carrying a lugsail, and costing the fishermen about £15. The most successful, because most assiduous, bold, and energetic, followers of this branch of marine industry, are the inhabitants of the Island of Bernera, Loch Roag, whose boats may be seen beating up amid the dangerous islets at the mouth of Loch Roag in the most tempestuous weather. Each boat carries a crew of four men, supplied with from twelve to twenty lobster creels, which completely occupy the boat, and give scant room for working, thereby much increasing the danger in rough weather.

CARLOWAY LOCH.

But our boat is swinging at anchor in Carloway "harbour," and as the sea is good and the wind favourable, we shall run down the rugged, dangerous, rocky coast beset with sunken "boes," and see what Neptune will send us to-day. The creels are shipped under the thwarts, about the bow, in every conceivable part of the available space; the mast is stepped, and, as the sail is set, we slide round the rocky point, and are soon running out the well-sheltered inlet known as Carloway Loch.

As we approach the mouth, a halt is made to raise the spiller line set overnight, in order to secure bait for the creels. Anxiously hook after hook is watched as the line comes in hand-over-hand, with an occasional gurnard or flounder to repay hours of trying labour.

Sufficient bait is now secured for the day's fishing, sail is again set, and we glide past the " bo " at the entrance, and so through the Sound of Cragum—that sound through which the sea seems always rushing like a mill-race, and where so many stiff pulls on a lee shore, against wind and tide in trying weather, have

tested alike our muscles, our endurance, and
our tempers. But we leave these adjacent
grounds for fishing in rough weather, and our
boat dances merrily past the Raven's Cliff, the
Rock of Scarts, and the many other beetling
precipices and breaker-haunted "boes" that
fringe this savage coast. At length we reach
the entrance of the open, unprotected sea loch
of Garnin, having baited our traps on the way
by fixing half a flounder or a gurnard in the
centre of the trap, so as to swing in an enticing
manner in the haunts of the aristocratic Mr.
Lobster.

The boat is now brought as close as possible
to the rocks by the aid of the oars, and a spot
chosen where a forest of thick-stemmed tangle
waves its broad leaves to the rocking of the sea.
The trap is lowered by a stout cord about fifteen
fathoms long, supplied with pieces of cork at
intervals of four or five feet along its whole
length, so as to keep it clear of the seaweed,
and a large cork buoy at the end with some
distinguishing mark, so as to be readily recog-
nised amid the ever-tumbling Hebridean sea.

Care must be taken to watch the state of the tide, so that the creel may be reached at all times. The very nature of the occupation directs the fishermen to the most dangerous localities, where, in the event of a heavy sea, which may get up at any moment, it is a matter attended with great peril to lift the creels, brought still closer to the breakers at low water. But our creels are gradually extending round the loch, one after the other dropping among the inhabi- tants of the submarine flora, like a cage through a skylight, leaving us at liberty to pass a short time as we please until their cautious and highly sensitive lordships have time to examine their repast.

Here, close by us, is one of those extensive caves hewn out by the ever-toiling sea in the gneiss cliffs, and colonised by myriads of blue rock - pigeons — the strongest, swiftest, most active, and, let us add, most beautifully marked of the British Columbidæ. The clip, clip of their wings is ever sounding in our ears as we lie on our oars beneath the cliffs, and occa- sionally send a shot among them as a larger

flock sweeps past at racing speed and disappears up the dark entrance. Ever-watchful
sentinels are posted on the adjoining rocks to
give notice of the approach of suspicious characters, and the whole community gives one
the notion of a vigorous, sustained, regulated
animal life. No ordinary attack will deprive
them of their lives, as often they fly to a great
distance with wounds severe beyond description.

What has come over the blue beauties ? How
silently they drop from their stations and skim
along in hot haste, close to the water, towards
the nearest rocky shelter ! See that flock, borne
on the wings of fear, pass by us like the wind.
" Coming events cast their shadows before,"
and the taper wings of the bold blue hawk—the
peregrine falcon—cast their ominous shade from
cliff to wave and wave to cliff. Now floating in
circles—now chasing, with silent, pertinacious
speed, that unlucky little scapegrace from cliff
to sky, from sky to wave, skimming round every
projecting rock, or shooting suddenly aloft, the
victim finds the dread tyrant, with claws clasp-
ing in anticipation, outstretched beak, and

eager, bloodshot eye, ever following with that steady tenacity of will and unflinching ferocity that does more to keep the tyrant "lord" than strength of talon or speed of wing. Panting more with fear than hot haste, subdued more by terror than overmatched in strength of wing, under the shadow of the projecting cliff the victim crouches with half-closed anticipatory eye, and in a moment is borne aloft in the clutches of the foe.

Above us, on those rocky shelves, sit the cormorant and green shag in pairs, their long backs towards us, while their heads are twisted round in careful attention. Back the boat quietly till we get a shot; fresh meat is scarce among Hebrideans, and, when skinned, the "skart" is a most welcome titbit, the fishy taste being withdrawn with the oily covering, leaves a good-sized body to the consideration of a native fisherman's boisterous appetite.

Hist! what is that, Anish, sitting on the rock smoothing its whiskers like a rufous cat? An otter! an otter! Now quietly! Alas, a lobster buoy-rope stays the boat, and we only get a random shot as it trots up the shelving rock to the inner shelter of the cave.

One of these rocky caves fell in two years ago on a quiet day here, the roar being heard as far as Briersclit, ten miles off. The boats at sea were so startled by the sound that they had imminent fears for their beloved Lews, while the spray dashed over the tops of the cliffs. These landslips occur very frequently in the spring, and the whole west coast is being gradually undermined by the action of the sea. When they happen at night, according to the boatmen, it is very grand—a great display of fire and volumes of smoke, from the friction of the rocks, rising above the seething waters.

But it is time to return to our lobsters, so we shall leave the stolid-looking skarts for a time, and make an inspection of the traps. The tide is much lower, and the tangle-leaves are waving where the white breakers lately dashed. We must back the boat in carefully, and keep a sharp look-out for unexpected rocks, for the sea is a treacherous friend in the West. As buoy after buoy is caught by a hooked stick, and the heavy creels are pulled up, eager eyes are cast at them to see what may prove to be the contents. The interest taken in the high-priced, high-coloured lobster, with its formidable weapons, one snap of which will draw blood; the contempt expressed for the comparatively valueless crabs, and the wonder constantly evoked as to how they could crush their broad backs through the strong iron rings much narrower than themselves; the mirth provoked at the expense of the skipper, as the active lobster, snapping its tail, springs from end to end of the creel, are constant sources of amusement. Strange and interesting objects, too, are drawn up from the beds of thick brown tangle. Through this the minor sea-savages roam, or in its midst they lurk in search of prey. Here, curled round the rope, comes a sea-serpent, as the fishermen call the members of the harmless Syngnathidæ, those marine marsupials combining the form of the snake with the maternal characteristics of the kangaroo. There is a huge star-fish, with its thousand brilliant mouths, sucking diligently at the flapping flounder.

This still exhibits signs of life, although taken
on the hook two days ago, its nose and tail cut
off, its body slit half across on each side, and thus
fixed on the horizontal string. Now a large tangle
is drawn to the surface, bringing with it a piece
of the ocean bottom, round which its roots are
clinging. Over this numerous minute crustacea
are running to and fro, delicate acalephæ are
clinging in the hollows, and marine architects
have covered it with buildings, formed from
materials brought by the sea itself for the use of
its diligent inhabitants; then greedy molluscs,
huge-headed cotti, or perhaps a savage conger,
or even a daring cormorant descending from the
regions of air has plunged to a hopeless death in
that element, where it is almost equally at home.

What are you laughing at? Lift the creel in
quick, and take your oar; don't you see we are
almost on the spray-girt rocks! In comes the
creel, and a strong effort shoots the heavy boat
out of immediate danger, and gives us liberty to
examine the inhabitants, crouched one in each
corner, with others clinging absurdly to the
netting—huge crabs every one of them, dis-

gusted with life and with one another, looking
intolerably stupid and ashamed of themselves
for being so "taken in." Not one of the lot is ·
small enough to force *at any angle* through the
hole it had entered at! Cork after cork comes
slowly in as the last creel approaches the top
of the water. What an eager plunge! "I have
him!" shouts Anish, as he raises his delighted
face and displays a mighty lobster, his great
nippers hanging like the helpless fists of a
ploughboy on his way to church. Unable to
crush even one of his immense claws through
the doorway, he has clung to the outside of the
netting, ceaselessly endeavouring to force one
nipper through. We gaze with interest on the
"bloated aristocrat," who has hitherto been
insured his crusty existence through the success
of his aggrandising policy. Sever the muscle
of his formidable nippers, and carefully wrap
him in an oilskin, to keep the wind from his
· tender majesty! Lobsters have. to be taken
great care of, as they yield at once either to
a cold wind, a fresh shower, or a frost. They
are pugilistic, and must never be allowed to

combat with a neighbour, as both may lose their claws. One of the swiftest inhabitants of the deep, it must be carefully and rapidly secured. The bait requires to be good and well placed, as they can otherwise withdraw it cleverly without entering at all; or if the doors are not made carefully they can find their way out as well as in.

Once more the creels are all on board, the mast again stepped, and as November nights are long, and the wind is low, we must hurry from this inhospitable shore ere darkness come down upon us. The Bernera boats are returning home in hot haste all along the coast northward, from seaward as far as the rocky island called the "Old Man Mountain," and from every islet that thrusts its dusky head through the tangle beds of old ocean. Slowly we force our way through the water, amid the black, treacherous-looking rocks that fringe the coast; but ere long we are flying, close-reefed, through the Sound of Cragum, thanking our stars that we trusted not the wind, now rapidly rising with the falling night.

What with small lines and long lines always set for bait—creels constantly shifted with the shifting weather, from sea-exposed rocks to calmer inland bays—early afoot, so as to be first on the ground—out late, so as to watch their property—ready in a moment to row for dear life, or sit calmly by the rudder in the straining boat before the hissing wind—the life of a lobster crew in the West is no child's play, but to claim success must be formed of able boatmen and resolute men.

WHAT a glorious stretch for a donkey gallop! How Londoners out for a holiday would revel on such a magnificent expanse of the purest sand!

Broad Bay, the El Dorado of Lews fishermen, is at our feet, rolling in with every wave myriads of shells of brilliant colours, whose defunct ancestors, in all stages of disintegration, form the beach for some feet deep beside us. Many waggon-loads of the little beauties are lying piled up among the sandy dunes, to be burned down for lime. They have a "higher destiny" than their friends on the beach; like a country boy on his way to town, to be ground into mortar for the social edifice of city life. We prefer them where Nature flung them in such rich profusion, after handing over their late owners to the tender mercies of the famous Broad Bay flounder.

The extensive sand dunes close by are almost entirely composed of such disintegrated shells. Upon them the bent grows luxuriantly, and crawling all over them may be seen the bearers of little land shells (Helix) of delicate structure and varied colouring.

In the season this district produces a large crop of mushrooms, whose value is well understood by a few discriminating immigrants. The otherwise omnivorous natives, however, look upon them with horror and disgust.

To the right of the bay stretches the hilly peninsula of Aird—a narrow neck of deep bogland dividing Broad Bay from the Stornoway waters. Here, on the side towards Stornoway Bay, the remains of an extensive wood may be seen at low ebb tides. The cotters have been in the habit of repairing thither, at such times, for the roots of trees for firewood, and a friend exhibited a hazel nut procured from the same locality. This, along with various other indications, seems to point to a gradual sinking of the land.

Nowhere, so far as we could learn, are trees found of any large growth, but like the bit of natural wood still remaining on the Lochs district, merely a larger species of brushwood.

A deposit of fine clay on this peninsula is worked for tiles, and is of so good a quality that vases and figures of superior excellence, both as regards design and workmanship, have been produced by the accomplished manager.

Close by, on the summit of a hill, are the remains of an extensive stone circle; and on an opposite hill, about a mile off, another known as the "Little Stones," of which only one large stone remains standing.

Alongside the shore of Broad Bay, the waters of which have already carried away a portion of the ancient graveyard, strewing the beach with human bones, stands the ruined church of Knock. The graveyard is still in use, but is covered all over with the densest vegetation, breast high. There is no enclosure, and, although apparently the most aristocratic burial-

place in the Lews, is utterly disregarded. The
stranger may stumble over broken capitals into
the doorless church, and there find massive
monuments concealed beneath a rank vegetable
growth. We cleared away a mass of weeds
from one corner, that we might view the monument said to cover the last of the Macleods.
No inscription whatever could be found about
the kilted figure in a pointed helmet, with
cross-hilted sword and dagger, that commemo-
rated the last of a race whose star had fallen.

There were monuments of beauty and value,
but what desolation! Is it from the struggle
for subsistence concentrating their whole ener-
gies upon themselves, that the Lewsmen can
spare no care for the dead? Or does it arise
from sheer laziness and carelessness, and
account for their terror of the "spirits," whose
former habitations they treat with such neglect?
If they care nothing for the "tenement of clay,"
after the spirit has fled, let them raise no visible
records of contempt!

As we turn from the unsatisfactory survey,
our ears are lulled by the "rock" of the waves,

I

and our eyes freshened by the rolling bay. A noble bay, indeed, it is, and one on which the gazer can never tire to look, whether dwelling on the innumerable gifts of ocean spread along at his feet, or raising the eyes to the broader aspects of nature on sea and shore.

Skirting the coast northward, at one corner of the bay is the pool of Tongue, where the river of the same name enters. Near this is the tract of Tussock grass, acclimatized from the Falkland Isles, which seems to have found a congenial home. We will hurry over the sands, and skirt the coast-line, until we reach another point of interest and beauty.

About eight miles north from Stornoway, finely situated amid undulating downs, lie the farmhouse and shooting-lodge of Gress. It is acknowledged to be one of the loveliest spots on the island, lying, as it does, on the finest bay on the coast, and commanding pleasant prospects both seaward and landward from its cheerful green-fringed·garden.

On the shore close by is the fishing-station of Gress, giving life and animation to the

GRESS AND BROAD BAY

neighbourhood, and studding the waters with dancing boats, from the small cod and ling or stout herring-boat, to the more important-looking smack.

This place is interesting on several accounts, besides its own intrinsic beauty of situation and fertility, amid the omnipresent moor.

On the shore below the shooting-lodge, the entrance to a primitive subterranean dwelling has been recently discovered by Mr. Liddell, the tenant of Gress farm, who takes a keen interest in all antiquarian subjects. This has been followed up to a certain extent, and found to lead under the green before the house, but the bulging in of the rude stone walls renders further progress dangerous, if not impossible. Its form seems to have been the customary one with such dwellings. A very small entrance leads to a vestibule, and a short way up the narrow passage two small recesses in the walls were evidently made to allow of two passing. Some ten or twelve yards beyond these, the roof suddenly showed an open ascending space, as if a chimney had been built. This might have been another entrance, a stone laid across the top closing it up, as the ground beneath was beaten hard, as by the feet of those leaping down. Upon clearing away the sand, with which it was silted up by the force of the wind and sea driving it from the beach, a layer of dark-coloured slimy matter, intermingled with bones and other remains, appeared. Some depth beneath this a fine layer of white sand, such as is not seen immediately about, seems to have been spread as a carpet. Upon and among this the most ancient remains were found, honeycombed bones split to extract the marrow, with the rude marks upon them where they had been struck for this purpose. They were principally bones of sheep and deer, of a small species, as would naturally be the case with progenitors of the present native breeds. The tusk of a wild boar also showed up, and many shells of the " roaring bucky," still sticky with oil, from having been used as lamps, as at the present day in Zetland. We could not find among the natives any who knew of the employment of this shell in such a way in recent times, although up to a very recent date shells of various species played an important part among the domestic utensils of the Lews.

No cutting instruments, so far as we could see, had been found, nor flint implements of any kind. An old quern found was not among the more ancient remains. The only other stone showing signs of manipulation was a circular flat stone like a discus, that had evidently been chipped into a more perfect form: its use was not apparent. As flint is thrown ashore in considerable quantities by the sea, the total absence of implements of this, or indeed any other article, seems strange. The height of the interior passage must have been considerable, as it enabled an ordinary-sized man to walk almost erect, when the sand had been cleared away. Originally it would have been much wider than at present, since the bulging in of the sides has narrowed it.

Of remains of a presumably later date there is a specimen in a ruined dune, of large size, on the top of a hill two or three miles inland.

This tower would have commanded a view of the Minch and a great tract of moorland. It had been built of very large unhewn stones, and as usual with such erections showed no signs of lime.

About a mile along the shore from Gress is a fine specimen of a trap dyke running through the conglomerate, and entering Broad Bay, showing again on the other side the bay near Garabost. The sea has ground out the conglomerate from one side of the dyke, forming one of the innumerable caves along the coast. The trap stands up like a huge black wall of great width and height direct from the sea on one side, the other being connected with the curving coast-line. It is the finest example we have seen.

Still continuing along the coast, the land traveller is directed to a huge cave hollowed out of the conglomerate. This is an enormous excavation, dry at low water, but into which the sea soon returns to continue its vigorous mining labours. It presents a huge cavernous aspect from the sea, as the roof slopes gradually back until at the further end it meets the gravelly floor at a sharp angle. Close by is a broad natural bridge, also of conglomerate, through which the sea sweeps at high water. Indeed, the freaks of these energetic Hebridean waves seem almost inexhaustible.

A short way along the coast, about a mile from the station of Gress, the celebrated seal cave runs into the conglomerate for two hundred yards or more.

This cave is formed in quite the opposite manner from the opening near the great trap dyke, for in place of the pudding-stone being washed away, here a large trap dyke has been cut away straight into the land. This has left a beautifully clear-cut sea-cave the whole width of the dyke for sixty yards from the entrance, thence it is so narrow that only the very smallest boat can proceed farther. Some way in it again widens into the furthest cave, which is high and roomy, with a gravel beach on one side.

The water is deep and clear, the rocky sides cut straight as walls, and studded under water

with many large sea-urchins. It is a favourite
resort of seals, and one rose with a splash
close by our boat, retreating into the further
recesses of the cave, where we were unable
to follow.

Altogether it is one of the finest and most
beautiful sea-caves to be seen, and although
not so imposing outside, is, in our idea, a much
more imagination-stirring and weird-like cavern
than the more celebrated cave of Staffa. No
one visiting Stornoway should ever leave without seeing this great natural curiosity, when
a few hours is sufficient to bring before the
bodily eye as charming a haunt of sea-nymphs
as ever startled the brain of a poet into dreamy
activity.

The road is continued past Gress, and ascends
a long sloping hill; from the top a fine view can
be had over the Bay and across the Point of
Aird to Stornoway Bay. The bold hills of
Harris bound the view towards the south, and
beneath us a long, sweeping, undulating green
land repays the labours of the husbandman.
The soil is greatly composed of that valuable

FROM PIGEON CAVE, GRESS, AT LOW WATER.

shell sand which, under judicious management, becomes so fertile. It has a fish-furnishing, friendly, fertile sea alongside, such as is of rare occurrence in the Lews; and the general impression left on the mind, after a survey from the highest point of the road, is that of a pleasant, open, cheerful, green, breezy land of milk and porridge, if not of milk and honey.

Gress itself lies snugly at the foot of the slope, and shows signs of steady and continuous improvement; but, as usual in the Lews, wherever the vicinity of a homestead shows money expended, it is the money of the tenant.

Still on the way to Tolsta, we descend the northern side of the hilly road and reach a fine valley running down to the sea, containing a little community of cotters. After a long ascent we reach the village of Tolsta, occupied by a mixed community of fishers and cotters, although situated at a considerable elevation over the sea. A steep road, a mile or two in length, leads to the station. The road continues on to a farmhouse, about a mile past the clachan, occupied by a hearty Yorkshireman. It is an agreeable situation, although terribly secluded, with undulating green fields down to the rocky seaboard, and rolling hills closing in the scene. Even in the opinion of its Southern tenant, it only requires a good sprinkling of plantations to be delightful. The view is cheerful, and enlivened by numerous sails that dot the neighbouring sea; but the place has no shelter from the gales, which sweep away everything, except the cobwebs of centuries that conceal the value, and hamper the activity, of the native mind.

A rocking-stone is poised on the top of a hill about a mile off. Although estimated to weigh thirty tons, it is said to be moved with ease.

On the way back to Stornoway we pass Coll, a farmhouse amid rolling sandy pastures sweeping down to the sea. It is placed on a little rising ground between two pleasant valleys, and commands a lively smiling prospect both landward and seaward.

NESS.

I F the Lews may be said to be pre-eminent in anything besides peat and ponds, let us give it the palm for getting up a big wind on the shortest possible notice : while to feel this wind to the utmost possible advantage, or disadvantage, go to Ness.

The district of Ness is a great plain extending from the Butt of Lews down to Barvas, without any elevations of consequence. This gives free scope for every wind to dance over its surface, striking a cold chill into strangers and energy into the aborigines, and rendering it in winter *de facto* a howling desert. "Uninhabitable," would be the verdict of any one brought to view the suitability of such a wretched tract for the habitation of workers either on sea or land. Not a sign of a natural harbour even for boats, vicious waves hissing and sputtering at the surly cliffs, whose rocky sharpshooters are thrown out to meet them; the bullying wind in its restless ferocity ever stirring up strife between them. Meeting the wild Atlantic as it hurls its mighty flood into the stormy Minch, the rugged Butt of Lews thrusts boldly forward its stubborn front, and like the Highlander who fought so manfully for a crooked sixpence, defends courageously its bleak expanse.

And yet this inhospitable-looking tract may be said to be the most prosperous out of Stornoway. About two miles from the Butt towards the East is the fishing-station known as "The Port" of Ness. It consists of an opening in the rocks a few yards wide, up from which a pavement has been laid by the laird to enable the fishermen to draw up their boats. This is all their harbour. Out of it no boat can be launched, even on the calmest day, without the men pushing them out up to their waists in water; remaining in this wet condition during the whole time at sea, which

NESS HARBOUR.

is often prolonged for two days. On returning,
they are again obliged to leap into the water,
to remove mast, oars, and ballast, and then,
after a hard day at sea, pull their boats high
and dry up the paved beach. The severity of
this labour is very great, and the men are said
to age rapidly under it. When at sea these
men often spread raw cod-livers on their
bannocks, and at all times consume a great
quantity of livers. This doubtless assists them
to endure long exposure in wet clothes: the oil
alike supplying heat to the system and lubri-
cating the lungs so as to secure them against
cold.

Above the Port, on the top of the cliffs, the
fishing-station, curing-houses, &c., are built;
and from this point the main road leads off to
Stornoway. Along this, for three miles from
the Port, stretches a continuous line of huts,
without a break, mostly placed well back from
the road, with the household peat-stack between.
Then to Skegersta on the one side and Lionel
on the other, two roads, to right and left of the
main, are likewise lined with evidences of the

possibility of a numerous population drawing
nourishment from this hopeless-looking domain.
Whence this numerous body of people draw
subsistence appears, at first, a difficult problem;
until we find that their fishing-boats are very
numerous, that they have enterprise to purchase
them from the curers, energy to fish under the
most adverse circumstances, pluck to go to sea
in weather such as the Western fisherman would
not face, and sufficient skill as boatmen to bring
them bravely through it. In the current sweeping round the Butt, the ling and cod are found
to be both numerous and good, and but for the
severity of the weather would well repay the
fishermen's labour. Even with all disadvantages
the Nessmen generally show a good average
fishing per boat—say three thousand ling. Besides the money value of these to be obtained
from the merchant, they are allowed to take so
many cod home to their families; while the
heads, the skate, dogfish, and fish-roes, contri-
bute to the sustenance of the household. The
bones provide titbits for their ponies and cattle,
the livers light their dwellings and supply occa-

sional "cod-puddings," and the garbage is carefully removed to make a compost for their lots.

Thus a successful fishing is a valuable source of profit to the community ; and a winter free from gales, especially easterly gales, which force the men to abide on shore, is looked forward to with anxious hope.

A good fishing will give each man from £15 to £20, besides otherwise benefiting the house-keeping. This, added to what is gained at the Wick fishing, with the assistance of meal and potatoes raised on their little lots, is amply suf-ficient for the simple wants of a Lewsman.

The soil is a rich loam, and raises capital crops with the help of seaware and fish-garbage ; but the harvest, dependent upon the weather, is very uncertain.

But it is ridiculous to suppose that the fisheries, as at present conducted, are alone capable of supporting such a large and rapidly increasing population. Besides, the people will not emigrate, as they declare themselves unwill-ing to leave their friends so long as they are happy and able to support themselves. The feeling of the majority of the people was plainly stated on the occasion of a late meeting to promote emigration to New Zealand, when a native arose and stated, that if the laird gave the land in lots to the people in place of to the sheep, there would be no necessity for emigration. A large body of cotters inhabiting several clachans were exported *en masse* to America some time ago, but still in this parish there is an increase of several hundred since the former census.

This is a question we have touched upon elsewhere, but it is here pertinent to ask *cui bono?* as to this emigration. One can understand the Duke of Sutherland depopulating a region for his own convenience or the cotters' social progress, but to send away a handful of people who will be immediately more than replaced by the natural increase does not seem a very masterly proceeding. If the vast body of human beings, over whom a purchasing proprietor assumes a serious responsibility, are willing to remain and make the most of their native land, it is his sacred duty to enable

them to do so as far as lies in his power. To
give them sufficient tracts of land to support
their families, for their own happiness and the
good of the State,—to endeavour to open up
whatever resources his property may possess,—
and to lease portions of his waste lands to such
cotters as are willing to improve them,—is as
much a moral obligation as furthering the education and social prosperity of those to whom
he owes a great part of his income. To export
several hundreds out of a country population of
twenty thousand, and endeavour, by starvation
on small crops, to force the remainder to follow
their example, is too paltry a policy to be cha-
racterized as a policy at all. When a capitalist
leaves money-making, and assumes the respon-
sibilities of a landed proprietor, a large interest
on money invested ought distinctly to become a
secondary consideration, subservient to the wel-
fare of his dependants, seeing he has voluntarily
assumed their management.

No one can view without astonishment those
long ranges of miserable dwellings, with their
happy inmates, and those ranges of peat-stacks,

representing many a gathering of neighbours to
the cutting, and many a "caley" over the con-
suming in the long winter nights. When the
simple elements of this happiness are considered, the natural verdict follows—" man wants
but little here below," excepting that "contentment which is great gain."

Let us step over this bank of turf and endeavour to see outside of this row of huts, often
two deep. It stretches on thus down to the
Port; but now we are outside we can see
about us.

Towards the north—why do you start? it is
only a few hundred blue pigeons rushing past
with their tireless flight, and blue and white
plumage dancing in the sun—to the north you
see the lighthouse standing on the edge of the
cliff, and blinking at Cape Wrath across the
Minch. It is a steady, respectable light, with
no particular enemies except the neighbouring
cave-dwelling starlings, that are caught in great
numbers by horsehair nooses fixed around it.
On revolving lights birds of all kinds are destroyed by driving against the glass, but a

steady light does not allure them to destruction, but gives notice in advance. To the west may be seen the famous hole in the rock to which the celebrated hawser was fixed that dragged the Lews from Europe, and thereby hangs a tale. The white patch in the dark rock, caused by the sea breaking through it, may be plainly seen from the road. Between the lighthouse and this hawser-hole stretch the rocky cliffs of the Butt—veterans scarred and disfigured in many a battle with the raging restless foe beneath.

Pigs! we exclaimed, as a grumph was heard from an animal rarely seen in the West. Yes, pigs! Ness has gone into pigs greatly of late; upwards of two hundred were exported this year, and a trade in this species of live-stock is quickly springing up. So the Highland dislike to the unclean animal, so common here, is giving way before the conclusive arguments of remunerative prices.

The men one sees about the Port are tall, big-boned, and powerful; the women buxom, stout, and hearty; the children numerous and active. But there is an unmistakable difference between this fair-haired race and the population of the West. They are taller, but not so stout; the women not so pleasant-looking, nor the children so bright-eyed and quick.

Let us enter the handsome schoolroom lately erected by the laird, and examine the state of mind and body of the scholars. We find about eighty boys and girls assembled, of all sizes and ages; some few cleanly dressed, and some six or eight who can read tolerably and cipher passably. Their teacher can at least speak English, an accomplishment few of the other teachers in the Lews seem to have acquired. But the education received is truly of the most elementary description, and, so far as we could see, the bulk of those present would never be reasonably well acquainted with the three R's under the present system. How could this be otherwise, when many have to come a good way to school, and any excuse is sufficient to detain them at home? Then when spring comes they are kept away to work in the fields, and help the females at their various labours, or the men in their preparations for sea. During the summer the visiting clergyman finds sometimes only two or three, and on one occasion, with a great effort, five were brought together to meet him. So with a very good schoolroom, and houses accompanying for resident master and mistress, the education disseminated therefrom is a mere farce. The Education Act has startled them, however, since we were there.

Standing on the rocky cliff called the Butt of Lews, overlooking the wide expanse of ever-shifting sea dashing its spray to our feet, all around skim the stout skiffs, manned each by six boatmen, in search of the precarious "el Dorado" which so often fails its most assiduous courtiers. Howl as you please, bully as you please, but yield us up your treasures!—and from Cape Wrath or the Skerries, to the far western banks, the deep must yield up its riches to the ceaseless assault. Five thousand souls, slumbering under the roots of the barley, wake every morning and turn to the east as anxiously as Parsee to the rising of the sun—

as seriously as Mohammedan towards the tomb of the prophet. How is the wind? That momentous question, to those who go to sea in open boats, is on every lip, and an Argus-eyed meteorological society watches every swirl in the sky.

On the rocks beneath us the pigeons are flitting to and fro in ceaseless activity, and an occasional cormorant or green shag springs from an overhanging cliff headlong into the deep. The gulls are skimming around us with suspicious rolling eye and irritating screech, or, gathered in a squalling, fluttering crowd, fight over some stranded titbit; while the sea now creeps like a treacherous tiger and laps the base of the cliffs, now springs with half-muttered growl to the weather-beaten summit.

UIGE.

UPWARDS of thirty miles from Stornoway, by Garynahine, lies the district of Uige. Although so much farther off than Shawbost or Carloway, it is nevertheless much nearer, so far as facilities for communication and elements of civilisation are concerned. Indeed, it is rather amusing to observe the airs of conscious superiority assumed by the people of this part, in their intercourse with the "barbarians" to the north of Garynahine.

A well-laden fishing-boat bound for Valtas is rocking on the beach at Loch Carloway; let us step on board and cross over on a visit to this famous district, by general acknowledgment the most picturesque in the Lews.

The stout boat before the stiff breeze soon

enters the narrow sound between the islands of Great and Little Bernera, on the latter of which at one time stood a chapel of the "black ladies," or nuns. As we proceed to the narrowest part between abrupt cliffs, with just room enough to enable a good boat to pass, under our keel may be observed extensive beds of Zostera marina, covering that portion of the sound bottom that lies opposite the snug, half-concealed, little farmhouse of the kindly "King of Bernera."

On emerging from the sound, fine sandy beaches lie on either side, on which the sea rolls heavily, carrying with it numberless habitations of the various molluscs that entice so great a variety of fishes to the neighbourhood. In front a circle of rocky islets, mostly white with the dashing spray, seems to prevent our further progress. Slipping through between two of them, however, we are soon crossing the other branch of Loch Roag that separates Bernera from Uige. Rapidly approaching the western side of the sound, we turn south and run down the shore of Pabba Island, a great resort of wild geese. With difficulty we double the southern point of the island, and run into the little roadstead of Valtas.

On arrival one is struck with the apparent fact that in this populous district there are plenty of men but no habitations. But when the eyes can be withdrawn from the magnificent sandy beaches stretching all around, and the neighbourhood carefully scanned for signs of human dwelling-places, a few can be with difficulty distinguished from the surrounding hillocks, amid which they are cast higgledy piggledy. Now we have scrambled ashore, over the slippery seaweed, and are stumbling up the sharp rocks, rendered still more dangerous by the still sharper shells of the limpets and barnacles, and, at length, are following our guide to the primitive dwelling, sunk somewhere amid the rocky knolls.

The impression given is, that no one could be seen for a hundred yards in a straight line anywhere in Uige. It is all "heighs and hows," up hill and down dale, and as few would care to build on the top of a hill in this gusty land,

the dwellings are necessarily unobservable until
you are close upon them. In nothing, however,
do they differ from those in other parts of the
island, except that more of them have rooms
completely divided from the cattle by a wooden
or stone partition. This shows that the people
are more prosperous as a rule, of which there
is no question.

The close proximity of this district to the
fishing-grounds enables the men to take instant
advantage of good weather in the winter, when
the fish also approach nearer the shore. At
the same time, as the fish always come from
the west, the fishermen here procure the first
attack on the shoals of fish—a very great advantage, and one obtained without the severe labour
necessary to those who have to cross from
Carloway.

Added to this, the blessed sands entice
myriads of flat-fish to their vicinity, and, as
it were, place in the hands of the fishermen
the best bait for ling, seeing the smallest boats
at any season can readily set spillers in pro-
ductive fishing-grounds.

This never-failing supply of bait for all kinds
of fishing, the incitement to exertion of resident
native curers who will not supply boats to lazy
or unskilled fishermen, and the ready access
to the fishing-grounds, soon tell in the large
takes of fish; bringing comfort to the fisher
families, habits of industry to the men, who
find their activity rewarded, and a general
brisk energy not to be found in the less fortunate districts.

A good many small tenant farmers add to
the prosperity and activity of the place, and
cause the small storekeepers to be in better
circumstances, and more enterprising; while a
regular postal service once a week to Stornoway, and the continued passage to and fro of
merchandise, bring the people into more direct
contact with civilisation than those dwelling
in the less prosperous villages northward.

Besides these fishing facilities and good
pasturage for sheep, Uige possesses more
natural features of interest than any other
portion of the Lews. Its splendid sandy
beaches, stretching along the coast for great

distances together, have already been mentioned, and are naturally the most prominent
objects to one arriving by sea. The bold bluff
of Gallon Head towards the north-west is a
point worth visiting, breasting the Atlantic, as
the Butt does towards the north. From this
a splendid vista of sea-beaten coast is visible
on either side; while seawards the Flannan
Isles, or Seven Hunters, seem just beside us,
and the more distant island of St. Kilda is
distinctly seen, sitting solitary in the watery
wastes.

North from Valtas is a fine example of those
large caves with which the Hebridean coast
is studded. The mouth seaward has been
banked up by huge rocks fallen from above,
and smaller boulders thrown up by the waves.
By clambering down the cliff it may be entered,
when the visitor can proceed in a great way
under the fern-fringed roof, until he finds himself lost in the dark among pigeon-haunted
peaks. Gladly will he return to the rays of light,
thrown in through the wide opening, now like
a little window far above him. There is a weird,

wild feeling which creeps over the rambler in
such rocky chambers that operates powerfully
on the imaginative Celtic mind, producing many
a tale of superstitious wonder, never absent
from such spots in a Celtic land.

Turning south by the only road to Valtas,
lately completed, we skirt the sea over great
rolling sandy downs. A mile or two brings
us to Meavaig, where the Free Church of Uige
is situated, a private road a mile long leading
to the minister's house. Skirting the sea from
the church, the new road enters the glen of
Meavaig, between bold and shapely cliffs. This
is considered the most picturesque walk in the
Lews, the road winding between advancing
and receding cliffs, with rugged rocky elbows
seemingly just lifted from the corresponding
green hollow on the opposing side, extending in
a pleasantly varied series for about two miles.
It reminds us much of the celebrated pass of
Keimanaigh, on the road to beautiful Glen-
gariffe.

Along the summit of the hills to the right,
the old road passes, leading to the Free Church

by a break-neck descent, trying even to a pedestrian, but which, we were assured, the native vehicles were at one time obliged to pass.

On emerging from the glen the deserted church of the Establishment stands on the hill, over the manse of Balnakill, at present occupied as a shooting-lodge, and bordering a vast sandy bay. Onwards, past several sheep farms, the road proceeds, until it halts twelve or fourteen miles off, opposite the populous little island of Scalpa, adjoining the mainland of Lews, containing twenty or thirty families, mostly engaged in the lobster fishery.

The sheep on the farms we are passing are exceedingly good, this being the best sheep-grazing land in the country. They ought certainly to be valuable, for the sheep on that little farm we have left behind us have replaced a hundred exported families.

But, although seemingly favourable for stock in the neighbourhood of the sea, we are no longer in a land of knolls but of mountains. Rude, bare, rocky peaks, one behind the other, stretch away to the south, and command the attention. The road clambers wearily along the vicinity of the coast, and becomes more and more irregular as we proceed. Before turning to the south we see on our right, amid green knolls, the clachan of Mangersta, whose inhabitants ere this will have been allotted fresh fields and pastures new in the vicinity of Carloway. The land they have is well suited for sheep, but their crops are rarely either grown or gathered in good condition, exposed as is their sandy soil to the full severity of the climate.

Wild cliffs stretch southward from this towards Harris, becoming more rugged as we proceed. The interior is a labyrinth of mountains rising gradually from the coast, vainly attempting to protect themselves from the blast by a thin layer of peat or moss.

A mile or two from the terminus of the road there is a wayside school, attended by about fifty scholars. It is conducted in that ordinarily fatal way of an absentee teacher attending college and leaving a substitute to conduct it on a pittance. Yet, in spite of the admitted faults of the system, through the strict supervision of the Free Church minister of Uige, who takes a personal and active interest not only in all the schools but in all the scholars in his district, we found the standard respectable. The scholars had a fair average knowledge of the English language, and the rudiments of a general education, showing how the conscientious discharge of an onerous duty by one man may improve the prospects of a whole community.

We found the people of Uige generally much more conversant with English than were the other outlying districts, and the church showed a large proportion of "comfortable" people, rationally dressed. The children, too, were of a more refined and civilised type than we found at Ness, more resembling those about Carloway district; showing less of the rude Norse, more of the sensitive Celt.

The charm of this land—and, believe us, it has a distinct hold on the affections of all visitors as well as natives—consists in the wild and solitary, yet distinctive, beauty of sea and land. Numberless lochs set in moorland, little heather, endless rain, clachans indistinguishable

from the rocks by colour or elevation; yet, as
one constant visitor remarked in the late
autumn, the land never looks so dreary as a
leafless forest land. The sea ever gives life to
the scenery, and satisfies the mental demand for
breadth, thus enabling the mind to turn and
make much of the lesser objects of beauty,
requiring closer and more familiar observation.

Let us turn from this sea-loch of Meavaig,
with the green shag, and white-breasted
goosander bobbing suddenly up on its surface,
as suddenly to disappear; with guillemots and
razorbills sailing slowly oceanward in soft-
breasted pairs, and little Highland cattle hurrying along its beach to luxuriate on the seaweed
—let us clamber up the neighbouring rocky
hill, and hurry over to the sea-trending valley
before the driving gale, and we shall at least
see one of the attractions of Uige.

Beneath and before us stretches a half-drained
loch, with the wind hurrying shadows over the
yellow reeds, that now rise everywhere through
the still waters, and throw their restless
shadows in the blue. Beyond, the sweep of the

L

Reef sands curves gracefully in the distance.
Swarms of gulls of half-a-dozen species, among
which the black-backed tyrant is conspicuous,
are shrieking and squalling, tumbling and
stalking all about. The blue sea is rippling
quietly on the sand, and the immediate view is
bounded by the circle of rocky islets that
enclose the Valtas' waters. A flock of grey
plovers is skimming above us, wild ducks are
harbouring on an islet amid the reeds, or
" prospecting " quietly around it ; and, as the
sun throws brilliance into the colouring on sea
and land, and cloudland, the kaleidoscope, turns
on its varying views, we feel that Ultima Thule
has not been forgotten in the creation of the
beautiful.

If such a thought had for a moment possessed
us, we had only to continue down to the sea
over the bent-covered sandy knolls, and view
the beautifully delicate shells everywhere covering the surface. Mostly of an exquisite pink, so
delicately constructed that, upon being loosened
from the sand, the airy beauty is at once seized
by the wind and whirled once more into the

waves. Each is seated on a sandy "tee," formed by the wind sweeping away the sand around it, as the storms of ages leave a perching boulder. Such exquisite flakes of ocean's pink petals we have never seen elsewhere, for although the other beaches of the country are plentifully supplied with shells, none equal these. We shall leave them to be raced over by the active little Dunlins, now stepping smartly and eagerly along beside us, and bear our heavier steps, so much less suitable for such a vicinage, back to the rocks and bogs.

It is only a year or two since the road was made to Valtas, and, indeed, the cotters as a rule are averse to roads. When it was proposed to have one made to Gayshider, a little clachan some miles from Meavaig—where the people have fair lots—they were very much against it, in case the proprietor should visit them, and, finding out how comfortable they were, increase their rents!

When one of the ground officers * was riding

* "Ground officers" in Scotland are petty stewards, subject to the head steward or *factor*. The Lews *factor* is called *chamberlain* of the Lews.

on horseback along a newly made road, he bid "good day" to an old woman, a relative of his own, who was sitting by the way. "Oh, yes!" she replied, "it was a fine day before the like of you could ride past here before the like of me."

Every real or imaginary improvement is looked upon as a "dodge" of the factor to add to the cotters' rents; and as their real or imaginary rights have been all ruthlessly invaded, they naturally view every new movement with suspicion. The cotters, however, calmly endure any severity of government so long as they may be left in peaceable possession of their lots; and should heaven send them good crops of barley and potatoes, and the sea yield a plentiful harvest, they will bless the land where they can obtain fuel for the cutting and carrying, and sing dull care away over the winter's fire.

CARLOWAY, BERNERA, AND GALLON HEAD.

CARLOWAY.

OF some places, as of some people, it is hardly safe to trust the hand to write. Who can be trusted to indite an article on the wife of his bosom, or write without apparently uncalled-for emotion about the home of his childhood?

So is it with us in respect to Carloway, with its pleasant bay, its rambling clachans, its cheerful cliffs, and, last of all, the many friendly faces we left beside its rocky shore.

The Carloway River, a good-sized stream, runs into the sea-loch of the same name, a broad tract being left bare at low water where it enters. As it passes seaward it narrows and deepens, takes a sudden bend at right angles round a rocky bluff, and resumes its westward course.

In this bend, sheltered from the direct action.
of the sea, the fishing-boats lie at anchor, exposed, however, to severe squalls down the
gully from the river. The sea-loch is nowhere
very wide, and everywhere irregular and rocky;
but we understand it has been taken note of as
an excellent harbour for a British fleet, in case
of war with America.

The vicinity of the boat-anchorage has an
extensive slope carefully cultivated, and in
spring and autumn presents a pleasing and
picturesque appearance. Many brilliant shades
of green combine well with the tawny rocks
and blue waves.

Sea, cliffs, and clachans—nothing wonderful
—and yet, and yet it is a pleasant place. For
nature here, as elsewhere, has her gala days
when she dons her gayest apparel. Every one
who has written of the Hebrides has described
the terrific hailstorms swept along by a de-
moniac wind, that, more especially in the late
autumn and early spring, sweep over the
weather-beaten, tanned, and everlastingly em-
browned face of this sadly abused land. No

one fails to enter minutely into details of the hail, snow, sleet, and rain, now alternating during a single day, now giving their whole minds to their work during a whole twenty-four hours—not working steadily any more than the Celtic inhabitants, but with boisterous and recurrent pertinacity. All this is it not written in the chronicles of " Sixty-one," than whom few are remembered more kindly in the Lews ?

But who has described the Lews in its real spring? Not boisterous February or March, but when all nature suddenly awakes, like the half-torpid inhabitants from the long nights of winter, and rushes to its labour like a giant refreshed. It presses out the primroses, and many a lovely wild flower, over the faces of the cliffs, hurries the laggard ferns into life by many a lonely watercourse, and decks the late sad-looking country in a lively suit of varying green.

One who has only looked at the Lews in winter has not the remotest notion of what this dismal tract is capable. A week or two of suit-

able weather, and the growth is almost super-
naturally rapid and luxuriant. As there are
no divisions over most of the country from
harvest to seed time, the cattle and sheep
roaming uninterrupted over the land, every
blade of grass is cropped up by the more than
half-starved anatomies that wander eager-eyed
around. But, the seed time over, they are carefully tended on the neighbouring moors, and
the struggling vegetation springs with a bound
into activity and beauty. With what affectionate fondness do the lovely primroses and
purple rock-daisies nestle in every creek and
corner of those bold western cliffs, while the
scrambling silver weed looks over from the
edge of its bed, spread along the upper slope.
The dweller in the sunny South naturally sup-
poses we are in a flowerless wilderness, but
see what we are walking through now as we
stroll along the borders of this pretty little loch,
a few miles from Carloway, waving with flags
and decked all over with lovely water-lilies.
The grass is green and luxuriant, and studded
with orchis of the most brilliant purple and of

DALEBEG—LOCH AND BAY.

large size. Beds of the yellow iris cover the damper spots, and the marsh marigold grows in the little streams. The crowfoot, the silver-weed, buttercup, and yellow clover show every shade of yellow, while the sober gowan and white clover sit demure amid their more gaudy friends.

The many species of delicate grasses give elegance to the green banks, and beautiful ferns, amid which may be seen the stately royal, adorn and border the stream beside us. The forget-me-not refuses to be forgotten, and the presence of the thistle makes itself felt; while violets and variegated vetches contend for a subsistence with many a less known and less respected brightener of the wayside. The lovely eyebright and the flowering nettle, and even already an occasional sprig of the bell-heather, are peeping at us from the rocks. For this is the charming little green vale of Dalebeg, charming both on account of nature and human nature, and, like the shadow of a great rock in a weary land, the sojourner in the wilderness is ever sure of a kindly welcome in its hospitable shade.

Between Dalebeg and Carloway there is a
renowned and very extensive beach of disintegrated gneiss, unprotected in the slightest
from the rolling Atlantic, which hurls its hollow
breakers continuously over the dancing sand.
A valley of rich pasture leads down to the
bent-grown "macher" that borders the bay,
handsome soft-contoured cliffs closing it in on
either side.

For a few miles on either side of Loch Carloway lies the snuggest and warmest and one of
the most pleasing districts we have seen in the
Lews. Northward of this it opens out into a
bleak rocky moorland, swept over by every
wind of heaven. Southward it becomes tamer
and more contracted, with flatter land and a
confined inland sea. Here it is snug; bold to
landward, and open to seaward.

Numberless lochs in the neighbourhood
abound with brown trout, and those whence
the Carloway River is fed are well supplied
with sea-trout and salmon. These latter, however, never rise to the angler in the Carloway
River.

As a rule, the sea-loch affords few fish, more particularly when the river is high and the season has been wet, the fresh water seemingly driving out sea-fish.

In Loch Roag, outside, however, a fair quantity of fish may be taken at most seasons, and few more picturesque sea-coasts can be found to set a drift of hooks along.

Let us run out and set our spiller line, and toss our black buoys on the wave, take careful bearings, and tack about for an hour or two. Our companions at sea are stupid guillemots, or quick-witted, sprightly, elegant sea-pigeons. The "bishop," or great northern diver, laughs and disappears as we seek to approach him, or an eider duck on a visit from the Flannan Isles tempts us in vain from our course. There a long-necked cormorant goes hurrying past with its strong inelegant flight, or a solan goose stops in its sailing course, and drops headlong with a splash into the deep. With what force the goose descends! On one occasion a boat was on its way from St. Kilda, when, it is said, one of these birds miscalculated its progress, and, in place of dropping on its prey, went crash through the bottom of the boat. The boatmen found it so jammed in that they left it sticking through the planks until they reached the shore.

But see that strange turmoil on the waters! A large flight of gulls are tumbling over one another again and again, in their frantic endeavours to get at a shoal of young herring. Not until we row right up to the spot do we observe any assistants, but on arrival we are amused to see the heads of dookers shoot funnily up, with a startled expression, from under the water all about us. These had been diving amid and under the shoal, whose silvery jackets thus rudely shaken off were dancing all through the surrounding waters. The gobbling gulls, unable to follow the prey under the waves, hastened to take advantage of the assistance thus providentially afforded them. The wild screeching and rude jostling and tumbling of the gulls was most ridiculous, and the whole flight might have been covered with a blanket, so close were they atop of one another during their rivalry.

We have time still to run along by the
bold cliffs, with now a natural bridge, now a
huge cave, now an isolated rock like a fortalice;
or, tacking about again, run across Loch Roag
to the island of Little Bernera, with its beautiful
beaches and rich pasturage. The prevailing
shells here are of the genus "patella;" about
Stornoway the most common genus is "car-
dium." The varieties of both are great. Look
at the bent turned into compasses! some one
calls out; and sure enough the stiff-pointed
grasses growing through the sand have been
caught in this eddy by the strong wind, and
the points have described beautiful circles in
the sand all about! Lazy herons are flapping,
active sandpipers running, and curlews are
as fond of hearing themselves screeching as
young ladies just "finished" from a boarding-
school. But our buoys have been dancing
long enough on the waves, and we seek our
home.

Let us now turn landward. News has come
to the cottage this morning that the people are
gathering for the Carloway fank.

A stroll of half a mile over the moor, or rather constant leaping over peat banks, brings us to the green margin of a pretty little loch, dotted with clumps of reeds. By its side the stone fank is placed, where the cotters' sheep, grazing on the moor in the vicinity, are periodically gathered. We are first on the ground, so must wait for a time beside the little pool, with the rocky hilly moorland spreading away on every side, diversified by an occasional loch, and enlivened by the little Highland cattle of the cotters dotted here and there over it.

At length the people begin to gather, and when next we raise our heads from tales of other lands, we find quite a multitude of men, with occasional women and girls, sitting on the knolls around. But where are the sheep? Patience! Hist! there comes the bleating of the pioneers, and, ere long, the flock of the clachan, several hundred strong, or weak, makes its diversified appearance. Every age and sex, almost every species, indigenous or acclimatized, are there; from the aged Cheviot ewe, with scarce a tuft of wool left, to the frizzy, black-faced lamb.

On they come! with plenty of vocal music as they proceed, and at length are enclosed within the rude walls of the fank; a crowd of bipeds surrounding it outside.

Now commences the robbery of the innocents —the shearing of the various fleeces. If any accustomed to Lowland manners, or shearing on a farm, expect similar regularity and decorum, they will be sadly disappointed. Here are no wooden stools of open spars with the shearers seated in—waiting for the victims; but in two minutes a rush has been made into the fold by wild-looking, bare-legged men and strapping, handsome, laughing girls. Each of the cotter horde seizes his or her one or two sheep, and drags them, bleating and struggling, amid the furious and constant vociferations of all, to the grassy bank outside the fank. The legs of the bleaters once tied, a dozen shears are plied by as many parties, each more or less, particularly less, skilful; and the bank is ere long covered by prostrate scores of nondescripts being denuded of their coats, or awaiting their turns, neither silently nor patiently. One consolation to the humanitarian arises from the fact that most of the sheep are pets, accustomed to being housed with the family to which they belong. So that, however anxious for wool, and unskilful at procuring it, they rather fail on the side of kindness and extravagance than of economy and cruelty. The reckless wounds indispensable from shearing on a great scale, as in Buenos Ayres or California, are nowise possible here.

Ascending the hill alongside, we look down on the busy scene in the midst of the desolate-looking hills. The snip of the shears reaches our ears, through the shouting of the men, the shrill screaming of the women, and the piteous calls of prostrate mothers to their terrified and equally noisy offspring.

There, a spanking girl, gaily bedight, springs into the fank, and soon re-appears with a sheep under each arm. They struggle in vain in arms accustomed to swing on her hips a creel of peats, under the weight of which many an athlete of my acquaintance would stagger like a giant in drink. There, a bare-legged girl of ten speeds like a fawn after a startled run-away, and turns it lightly on its back, as if turtle-turning had been the business of her life. The freed and wretched - looking creatures, already stripped of their winter coats, rush bleating to the hills, the lambs helplessly seeking their comfortless mothers, amid the miserable and scattered parties spread over the neighbouring moorland.

Verily! if those excitable Celts did not manage to carry a sparkling interest into the very simplest affairs of life, could they dwell so happily and contentedly on this "floating peat"?

Near us, in the rolling land between Carloway and Tolsta Chulish, is the celebrated Dune Carloway. This is the best preserved of any dune we have seen in the Lews. These circular dry-stone Pictish forts, or places of security, are very numerous in this country. At least a dozen are in the parish of Uige, and many of them have formerly dotted the sea-coast as

M

far as Ness. They are generally built close by a freshwater loch, not far from the sea, and are always innocent of lime or mortar. Still they have been so strongly built as to reach the Lews of to-day from distant times, and would doubtless have done so in much better preservation but for the ready quarries they have proved to the cotters.

Dune Carloway is built on a slight elevation, overlooking a fine freshwater loch abounding in trout; while, at the same time, it affords a capital view over Loch Roag and out to the Atlantic.

On the road to Ness, a number of villages border the sea on the left hand, and a few ruined dunes are to be seen beside the lochs on the right. These villages merit observation from the peculiarity that they are built generally beside embouchures of " rivers." The sea, in almost every case, has thrown up a magnificent bank of gravel at the river-mouth, thus spreading it out into a freshwater loch, with this great gravel bank between it and the sea. On the top of the bank the fishing-boats of the community are ranged, while the river skulks round the corner seaward. This is quite a distinctive characteristic of this part of the coast. Beside Dalebeg, there is a cliff apparently of good granite, much used for millstones, which shows no sign of stratification. As the neighbouring formation, however, is gneiss, it does not seem exactly in order, any more than the weird tales told of its boduch-haunted environs.

The other day, we obtained the complete appurtenances of a veterinary surgeon. These consisted of a " serpent stone " and a serpent's head. The stone was simply a disc with a hole in the centre, and two plain circles cut out on it. Such are held in great esteem, are very rare, and their appearance is accounted for in various ways. The commonest account given is, that the hole in the stone is caused by the passage of a serpent through it, a Harrisman having found one on the way through. A more fanciful and complicated belief assigns their origin to nine times nine snakes passing continuously round a heather bush? An idol-breaker from the mainland insists that such stones were common at the end of the spindles formerly, in place of a swelling in the wood, or an extemporised potato, as at present.

However this may be, the people have great faith in these stones as a cure for cattle, when bitten by snakes, as well as in many other ills that bovine flesh is heir to in the Lews. One of these stones is placed in water, or water is poured over it, and then given to the cattle to drink. Only three or four were known to be in the Carloway district, and these were in constant requisition for swelling in cattle, and other ailments. In default of the stone, or as an additional security, the head of an adder tied to a string was used in the same way, and for the same purpose. Such heads were more common, and in constant use. Will Mr. Phené, who is acquainted with the Lews, claim these customs as a relic of widespread serpent-worship?

A medley of ancient superstitions and modern bigotry exists universally among the people. The boldest by day fear to go about at night, and endless tales of Boduchs, or spirits, distend the eyes of young and old round the peat fire. Here a water-horse revels in some roadside loch to the terror of the wayfarer. There, a "head" trundles along the hilly road all alone, and taboos the whole vicinity to travellers. Now, mysterious lights about the kirk disturb the repose of the whole community; and again, some stalwart fisherman wrestles with the "Boduch Mohr"—Satan himself—a whole night long on the moor, and "has never been the same man since."

You are passing along the road at Callarnish. Hasty steps are heard behind, for no one is so bold as to pass within a mile of the stones alone in the gloaming, and your company for the present is in urgent request. The pedestrian may have travelled in far lands. Were you afraid there? you ask. "Not in the least"— only in the dread land of his birth, darkened by the tales of the "cailliachs."

Then there are no musicians whatever among the people, as the ministers and elders as a rule proscribe such pure enjoyment. One lame lad at Shawbost had bought a fiddle to

solace himself during the long winter evenings, but the elders forced him to dispose of
it, and now not a man plays anything but a
Jew's harp among the natives of the west.
Indeed, only lately have they relaxed so far
as to have even dancing, and many ludicrous
scenes have we witnessed from the holy horror
of the elders. Everything that dark superstition and a severe creed can do has been done
to oppress the minds of the people; but Celtic
blood will show, and, with happy homes and
minds at ease, they are "merry and wise,"
in spite of all ghostly interference.

THE LEWS ANTIQUITIES.

ALTHOUGH geologically the oldest formation in Europe, the Lews must have been
one of the latest settled. We need not look here
for evidences of existence during the drift
period, or contemporaries of the cave-dwellers
of France or Southern England, for at that
time the Lews was either bound under an
eternal Arctic winter, or, sunk beneath the
waves, stranded the floating icebergs, and
received the boulder deposits from their melt-
ing decks. Along the west coast a continuous
series of rounded boulders, evidently of glacial
deposit, cover the land, and the forms of the
lower hills evidence the action of grim winter,
as it loosened its hold of our islands, and retired
struggling to the Northern wastes.

We shall not then seek for drift deposits, nor need we look for signs of the long-headed cave-dweller, for they might chase the mammoth or the cave-bear across what is now the Straits of Dover, but could find no rest for the soles of their feet beside the Barvas hills. If this race still survive in the Esquimaux, they must have crept northward by way of Northern Europe, probably at a time when the North of Britain was uninhabitable. At any rate, neither of this race, nor of the more modern people allied to the Lapps—who, according to Nilsson, were the keen-witted race who formed the "fairy bolts," lived in underground dwellings, and were rooted out by the more powerful Teutons—do we know anything here. Unless they appear in this story from Martin: " The Island of Pigmies, or, as the natives call it, the Island of Little Men, is but of small extent. There have been many small bones dug out of the ground here, resembling those of human kind more than any other. This gave ground to a tradition which the natives have of a very low-statured people

living once here, and called 'Lusbirdan,' *i.e.*
pigmies." Does this point to a remnant of the
Lapp race that had taken refuge in these
farthest outlying islets of Scotland, the Flannan Isles, or Seven Hunters? It is supposed
that this latter race were the builders of the
beehive dwellings and underground houses
found in various parts of the mainland. Does
this necessarily prove that the beehive houses
and underground dwellings of the Lews,
some of which have been recently inhabited,
were of their erection? We think not. We
do not see the necessity for dragging in Lapps,
or even Iberians, to build, although they may
have originated, any ancient dwelling on the
Long Island.

Let us take the population as it at present
exists. No one can doubt for a moment that
it is essentially and unmistakably Celtic. Indeed, in Scotland, at any rate, it is only necessary to look at the map, or read the statistics
of the country, to tell where a Celtic population is to be found. Is there a good fishing-
station, or an energetic centre of any given

industry :—you may safely affirm that Scandinavian or Teutonic, never Celtic, energy or
enterprise has originated and developed it.
The Celtic races, with the important exception
of the Cornish men—if it is an exception—never
seem to become thorough seamen. They are
tillers of the soil, to which in general they are
passionately attached. The Lews is no exception to this rule, as the Scandinavian settlement
is the only vigorous fishing community. Not
that Ness is the only Norse portion of the
Long Island, as the occupation of many hundred years has naturally left its stamp on the
inhabitants throughout the country. But out
of Ness the Celtic blood, which was necessarily
that of the women, has absorbed alike Northern
energy and Northern instincts.

Granted then that the present population is
Celtic, with a Norse admixture, we must reason
back from the present if in any way it can
explain the scattered and shattered remnants
of the past. First, as to their dwellings considered with reference to antiquity. These have
unquestionably, up till recently, diminished in

constructive skill and stability. This is to be accounted for by the great increase of population during the present century, and the far more subordinate position of the sub-tenants as compared with that they enjoyed under the ancient chiefs. Their shielings on the moor, in which the women spend a great part of the summer, are built exactly as the beehive dwellings, but of more perishable materials. In the vicinity of Shawbost there are still several of these stone-built and roofed beehive houses, occupied in the summer by the cotters; and one, in the immediate vicinity of Garynahine, shows the roof well built of large overlapping stones, so as to form a strong-built dome. Otherwise, however, it is the same as the numberless shielings spread over the island, with two low opposite openings into which to creep, holes in the wall for the milk-dishes— showing a pastoral existence—a rude chimney proving an advancement on the present erections, where no chimneys are found.

Thus we see that unmistakable Celts in modern times erect and dwell in beehive houses; the exigencies of the climate, the country, and poverty having carried these onward into modern life: reminding one of a street Arab standing, bewildered and out of place, on the threshold of a London ball-room.

Are they a natural product of poverty and necessity, or have they any distinct connection with the modern Esquimaux habitations and those of the ancient Lapp inhabitants of Northern Europe? Were they adopted from an exterminated race in previous possession, or brought north by the Celts themselves, as we find them also in Islay and elsewhere in the west? We have no data for any conclusions on this point, and without them speculations are valueless. Still, it is worthy of observation that stone implements are rare, and all we are acquainted with can be told off on the fingers. These may also be of very recent manufacture, as a people, so destitute of metal instruments even lately, would unquestionably use stone; and we were informed of stone hammers having been in use in the west within the century. An underground dwelling recently opened at

Gress, and containing quantities of bones split to extract the marrow, showed evident signs of having been inhabited long subsequent to the original habitation—say within two hundred years—from the freshness of the bones, which had yet been broken with stones.

Besides the ordinary black-house and bee-hive dwellings, a better class have prevailed. Take, for instance, the rectangular dwelling of good size, built on an island on a loch above Dalebeg. This must have been placed there for defence, as the island is too small to be of use either for pasture land or agricultural, so that the building must surely be some centuries old.

All these circumstances point to the belief, that in former times, as at present, the unprogressive Celt erected his human stye alongside the comfortable or lordly dwelling of the invading Teuton; that he may have done so for twelve centuries or twenty; and that speculations based on the probable age of such dwellings elsewhere must be received with great caution. Groping, as we are, in the dark at present for fragments of the ruined mile-

stones leading back into the past, it is more
important to read one stone clearly than to
jump to conclusions respecting twenty. We
shall, therefore, leave these perishable erections,
and see if we cannot read approximately the
more striking, if not more important, " mile-
stones " left standing by the way.

The most prominent of these is the megalithic
structure known as " Turusachan," or the Callernish circle. It is, following the survey, 13
miles due west from Stornoway, consists of
48 stones, and the highest point of the hill on
which it is placed is 143 feet above the
level of the sea. The circle is 80 feet above the
sea, 42 feet in diameter, with the centre stone
17 feet high. All are of unwrought gneiss.
Inside the circle, lying east and west, is a
cruciform grave, whose position the centre
stone may have indicated. In this chamber,
according to Dr. Stuart, were found fragments
of incinerated human bones, imbedded in an
unctuous substance apparently composed of
peaty and animal matter.

So far as the name goes the derivations are

arranged to suit the advocate who is analyzing it for a particular theory. Thus, the Druid theorist—"*call*, a circle, church, or temple; *airn*, of the judge; *geis*, of sorcery; *call-airn-gheis*, the circle or church of the Druidical judge. This shows why the circle was so large and so distinguished. And there is little doubt that, in the republics or states of the Hebrides and Orkneys, the population may have been nearly, perhaps fully, as numerous as on the plains of Salisbury and Avebury."

According to the Surveyor-general, *Callernish* is bleak or cold headland; *Callanish*, place of assembly for worship, or calling to prayer; *Turusachan* is a place of pilgrimage; *Tursachan*, place of sadness, sorrow, or weariness. But the Druid theory, that has held sway so long, threatens to succumb before the hard-headed examination of the modern scientist, and certainly the most probable reading is the first, and that, like Vaternish, Trotternish, or the many other headlands in the west, its name is a legacy of the Norseman. Considering that the Lews nomenclature is mainly Norse, this may be taken as granted.

Before proceeding to discuss the probable age of the temple we shall recapitulate a few of the theories that have been brought forward respecting it.

1st. Like all such megalithic structures, it has been claimed for the Druids, whose *temples* are not mentioned.

2nd. The Baal worshippers have claimed it as their own, from a fancied resemblance to the sun set on a stick, which they suppose to have been the original mode of symbolizing the orb of day, here transferred to a more imperishable material.

3rd. It has been suggested that it is a relic of Phallic worship, but this is altogether fanciful.

4th. The latest theory is that of Fergusson, who is delighted with the discovery that it is twin-brother to a chamber buried under a tumulus at New Grange in Ireland, from which it has been copied, and is, therefore, simply the tomb of a great chief.

5th. It is claimed for the Norsemen, who held the Isles in subjection for so many years; the neighbouring circles having been used as Things by the Scandinavians, as they have been similarly elsewhere until recent times.

We shall endeavour to bring together a few converging facts, and thereby arrive at some more definite notions of the object and date of its erection.

We shall not here combat the Druidical theory, as that is generally discarded; although any one who is acquainted with the extraordinary tenacity of memory of a comparatively uneducated people, who have no masses of light literature to dilute the homely vigour of their faculties, will be most unwilling to discard as valueless, alike inherited traditions and the deep impressions of a people as imbedded in their language. Still, although "to go to the stones" is to go to church, and the expression must have been long anterior to any modern notions of Druidism, grafted on the old traditions of their fathers, it may refer to a time when the spirits of the mighty dead were their gods, and their sepulchres the only temples.

If a place of worship, the independent testimony of the peat shows it to have been neglected for six or eight hundred years. Well! this is one slight datum to start from. Then as to the form, it is strange to us, that those who chased a resemblance even into the centre of a tumulus, did not observe that it was a plain, unmistakable imitation of an Iona or Irish cross. This cross is *sui generis*; peculiar, in Europe, to Ireland and the West Highlands; and is generally believed to be the Christian cross with an encircling halo. Here is a peculiarity pointing to its erection posterior to A.D. 565, when St. Columba settled in Iona, taking with him this peculiar form of cross. We are thus circumscribed in our inquiries, the probability being that its date is between the sixth and twelfth centuries.

If not in imitation of the Iona cross, it was probably merely the cruciform arrangement added rudely to the circle. This seems a natural explanation.

But both Scots and Norsemen were builders of megaliths. Was it erected by the Celtic inhabitants? It does not seem natural to suppose that a race accustomed to the elegant crosses of Iona would raise such a rude example: nor would a native race be likely to raise it to their own people when under Norse domination. Nor would the Celtic population raise such a Pagan memorial after the ruin of the Norse power in A.D. 1265.

What reason have we, on the other hand, to suppose it erected by Norsemen?

The other megalithic remains bear a close resemblance to those of Scandinavia, especially a fosse and circle near Garabost, surrounding the top of an elevation on which is a menhir and kist, closely allied to fig. 107, Fergusson's "Stone Monuments." Then Callernish evidently having been a circle with a cross rudely added; or else a direct copy of an Irish cross. Again, a large menhir near Barvas was erected in historic times by the Morrisons of Ness, a Scandinavian race, to commemorate a victory over the Macaulays of Uig: it is larger than the centre stone of Callernish. While we have just been reinforced by a description, by Dr. R. Angus Smith, of a place of the same name in Iceland, whose vicinity has likewise been honoured with the presence of an ancient temple.

The numerous remains of churches and nunneries over the Lews show that the country was early christianized, and completely under the rule of the priesthood. It is not reasonable to suppose that the comparatively refined Celts would exhibit such rude power so lately. A people pass from rude force into gradually weaker art, and when art dies they exhibit rude weakness, never rude power.

Consequently we are inclined to the Norse as the most probable agents in their production.

Basing our inquiries on this conclusion, let us see at what time they were likely to have raised them.

The Norse were nominally christianized in A.D. 1000; so that prior to that date a pagan people were not at all likely to raise a monument in imitation of those of their conquered subjects. More than this, the two graves discovered within the Callernish circle were cruciform, so far pointing to a Christian origin. This again narrows the probable date down to that period embraced between 1000 and A.D. 1263.

But although from the cruciform arrangement, both of the structure and the contained graves, the erection must be subsequent to the year A.D. 1000, still it cannot have been long after that date, as the Norsemen must then have become too deeply imbued with Christian precepts to erect such pagan memorials. It was during the eleventh century that the influence of this northern race was paramount among the islands of the west as far as Ireland, until King Brian, as the champion of the new faith, broke their power. If they had raised this structure towards the end of their sway, the subject race would scarcely have respected it, or left it standing.

So, in reviewing our position, we arrive at the conclusion that the evidence inclines to prove Callernish Norwegian. The name itself; its recently discovered Icelandic counterpart; the custom continued in the Lews into historic times by the Norse descendants; the evident imitation of a Christian cross by semi-pagan warriors, or its addition to the circle; and, lastly, the evidence of the superincumbent peat, which, although uncertain in itself, strongly corroborates the supposition that the stones were raised, in all probability, not earlier than the tenth century, nor later than the thirteenth.

We are inclined to fix the date as the eleventh century, the only one in which the pagan element would be likely thus to intermingle and combine with the Christian.

In a manuscript history of the Lews, written about the beginning of the century, there is an instance of the Druid theory creeping in. After detailing the received account of the Barvas stone, raised by the Morrisons after a battle with the Macaulays, when both parties were nearly exterminated, the writer subsequently interpolates, "yet some maintain that it was placed there by the Druids." As the writer (Dr. Macrae) was both a medical man and a clergyman, and so likely to be well informed respecting the received traditions of the people, such an interpolation is strongly corroborative of the belief that the Druid theory is of extraneous birth, and had then no foundation in the traditions of the natives. And yet Martin, a century previously, remarked that the tradition of Callernish among the people is Druidical!

The two or three small circles in the neighbourhood of Callernish may have been used as Things, or marked the occurrence of battles. Fergusson's argument against these circles being places of meeting, seeing they are wholly unsheltered in a boisterous climate, is of no value, seeing that even in these degenerate times the communions are held in the open air, the clergyman alone having a wooden box, while the congregation sit around on gathered stones.

Loch Roag must have been the snuggest and most convenient harbour in the north for the Norsemen, and its vicinity was thickly populated. All round its shores are numerous remains of dunes or brochs, and great tracts of land, now under peat moss, are said to display signs of former cultivation. A mild climate, secure harbour, immediate vicinity to what was formerly the best fishing - ground in the Hebrides, it was eminently fitted for the sea rovers. As the centre of population, at the head of the loch, and readily accessible by boats, it would be naturally chosen as a place of assembly for the delivery of laws, or otherwise.

The Menhir and Kist, near Garabost, surrounded by a fosse and stone circle, are evidently of purely pagan origin. The stones have been originally very large, and the centre kist has been opened in search of treasure. On the low hill opposite is a large menhir known as the "Clach Stein," the Gaelic having been prefixed to the original Norse.

Leaving the megaliths, we now come to the dunes or brochs, so numerous along the western coast. The MS. history previously quoted mentions the belief that these were dismantled by the Norsemen, having previously formed places of defence for the Celtic aborigines. Let us examine this belief.

CIRCLE AND KIST AT GARABOST.

In the first place they are never built with mortar,-but formed of well-fitting stones, and yet one or two of them are in tolerable preservation. The old churches scattered through the island have, on the other hand, almost entirely disappeared, although cemented with the most tenacious lime. If these so-called Pictish towers were so ancient as is generally received, would they thus have outlasted the more securely built and more revered sacred dwellings?

In many cases the people have used them as quarries, from which to build their huts, and in no case show any reverence for them whatever. The tales connected with these among the natives have reference to giants, *and these are furnished with Norse names.*

Again, where are the remains of the Norse strongholds? We know they held the Hebrides for centuries, and this would necessitate places of defence from the conquered subjects. There are one or two castles of comparatively modern date, but where else are we to look for the residence of the Norse rovers, if not to these strong towers?

The first conclusion we come to is, that they are not more ancient than the mortared ecclesiastical buildings already fallen to decay ; say those of presumably Culdee origin. We have no reason to suppose they could have outlasted them. Then by whom were they built ? Why such towers should be Pictish it would be difficult to explain, except that any inexplicable erection is at once made prehistoric. Are any such towers found in the Pictish or Dalriadic kingdoms ? What possible connection is there between these brochs and the known Pictish towers, such as that at Abernethy, the capital of the Pictish kingdom ? Such an appellation seems a mere begging of the question.

Then, if not Pictish, are they of Scottish origin ? If built by Celts, it must either have been previous, or posterior, to the Norwegian domination. If after the Lews chief had sworn fealty to the Maid of Norway, we should surely have had some knowledge of them, as we are then in comparatively historic times ; nor do we know of any necessity on the part of the natives for such strongholds.

Again, to what use could the inhabitants put
them? The only suggestion we have seen made
was, that they were places of shelter for the
adjoining villages in case of Norse invasion.
But they are too small to hold the inhabitants of
a village; and if villagers were thus to leave
their huts unprotected, their most natural as
well as most successful manœuvre would be to
betake themselves to the moors, where they
would gather strength by junction with their
neighbours, in place of cooping themselves up
in these little towers.

Now these towers are mostly in the vicinity of
the sea, and generally upon a small freshwater
loch or river; and around Loch Roag, which we
have seen was probably a haunt of the rovers,
they are more than usually numerous. Also
there is scarcely a loch on the way to Ness without its ruined dune.

We thus find that the district principally
infested by the sea-rovers is that thickly studded
with dunes. The same holds good on the mainland in the north-western parts of Inverness,
Sutherland, and Ross-shire, as well as in

Orkney. They are seldom far from the sea, as if leaning for support upon their galleys, and are just such towers as invaders unskilled in masonry might erect, among a hostile population. Too small to shelter a village population, they are sufficiently large to accommodate a handful of resolute men; and scattered along the seaboard would yield each other support while overawing the people.

If they had been built by the natives to prevent the landing of rovers, they would have been built still nearer the sea, and in very different situations; nor would they have required the immediate vicinity of freshwater lochs if secure of the sympathy of the population. Nor can any one who has examined them suppose them to be of the nature of guard or watch towers, as one can rarely be seen from the other, and a people afraid of incursions from the sea would surely have built their towers on eminences, whence the coming danger could be seen and telegraphed.

Indeed these considerations, together with the fact that the north and west coasts and the Isles are the districts where these towers most do congregate, as the Norsemen did formerly, and the traditions of giants inhabiting them with Scandinavian names, as the giant Glum in Uig, all point to a Norse origin. The only towers at all resembling them, of which we have knowledge, are those built by the early Norse settlers in Greenland, at Ericsfiord, settled by the Norsemen in the eleventh century, as mentioned by Hayes. We do not acknowledge their similarity to the Sardinian.

It is natural enough that a race of rude circle builders, whose possible Things are in the midst of the dune district, should have erected round towers of large unmortared stones, in which each petty chief might exercise as uncontrolled authority as in his war-galley.

It may be interesting to add the following note from Gardiner's " Indians of Chili : "—" Near the Andes several rest-houses at regular intervals were erected. They are built entirely of burnt brick, laid on lime, with a coped roof of some material supported by an arch which forms the ceiling. May not those remarkable towers, called dunes in Scotland, have been erected for purposes somewhat similar?" To this a friend replies, that as several are occasionally found close together the similarity is imaginary.

THE LEWS ANTIQUITIES,

THEIR SUPPOSED SABÆAN ORIGIN.

W E shall now discuss their claim to a more
ancient date of construction, before ever
a Culdee passed from Iona with tidings of peace,
or even before the gentle Galilean preached his
sermon on the mount.

Their claim to an Eastern origin cannot be
passed over in silence; but whether brought by
the Scythian-Sabæan worshippers or the Tuath-
de-danaan worshippers of Buddha, we are not
informed.

It appears to us that modern research tends
strongly to the belief that, from their cradle in
Asia the nations have spread east and west,
carrying with them a mythology in which the
combined reproductive and destructive powers

of earth and sky have been symbolized in the human body. It is the foundation of Buddhism; and with necessary modifications is found alike among all the non-savage nations east and west—from the Peruvians and Aztecs to the Scythians and Celts. This we here term Sabæan for want of a better word, in allusion to the original idea.

A writer upon Eastern subjects remarks upon the familiarity with which Christianity was regarded by the Buddhists of India; while historians equally acknowledge the peculiar readiness with which the Highlanders listened to its tenets. Just now a medical friend has stepped in from an examination of a collection of skulls, with the observation, " I was much struck with the extraordinary similarity between the skulls of the Hindoos and those of the Scotch, so essentially distinct from those of the Teutons."

Both these widely separated peoples possess the same contemplative and imaginative cast of intellect, and the Highlanders of Scotland, along with their Eastern garb, have ever been renowned for Eastern courtesy and delicacy of mind. It may also be remarked that the famous Celtic form of brooch cannot be distinguished in numerous instances from the brooches of Hindostan; while it has recently been observed by a traveller, that the long bone combs found in tumuli, etc., and hitherto unexplained satisfactorily, are identical with those still used in the Himalayas for arranging the threads in weaving; the same article being in use among the Aztecs in New Mexico.

Proofs are adduced that the Tuath-de-danaans, the Buddhist race supposed to have held Ireland for two centuries, were driven into Scotland, where they are said by Buddhist theorists to have left some sculptured evidences of their occupancy. They were again driven to the extreme North by the ruder Celtic people who followed them; but as they are said to have been a literate and comparatively cultivated people, they no doubt influenced to a great extent their ruder conquerors. Indeed, the character of the present Highlanders—combining, as it does, the love of music, song, and

Eastern grandiloquence with habits of delicate courtesy, and at the same time the Scythian passion for war and the chase—is exactly that to be anticipated from a combination of the Tuath-de-danaans and the Scythian warriors. We are told, "From the cities of Ur and Babylon, northward to the remote regions of Caucasus *and the Scythian nomades*, ... the infatuated nations adored the sun, the moon, and the hosts of heaven;" so that we may conclude the Scoti or Scythians were essentially Sabæan worshippers.

Again, it may be remarked that the circle at Garabost, so closely resembling a Scandinavian example, must also bear a great similarity to one on the battle-field of Northern Moytura, as figured in Fergusson and compared by him with the Danish. But Moytura has been claimed both for the Tuath-de-danaans and the Scandinavians, so that we are no further advanced in the inquiry.

Still, we must accept the *possibility* of a Buddhist race passing north from Ireland; so in the absence of any sculpture in the Lews

antiquities that we are aware of, to prove the
Buddhist kinship, we merely acknowledge the
argument for their post-Christian erection,
based on the cruciform arrangement, to be of
questionable value, the cross having been an
Eastern and pre-Christian symbol. Yet the
probability must remain in favour of the more
recent and modern derivation.

The towers, again, if built by the same race
as the round towers of Ireland, from having
been built without mortar must have been so
when that race was on the decline. O'Brien
suggests that these towers were internally provided with little platforms for placing rows of
images upon, as in Indian pagodas. This seems
to be the case. In connection with this idea
we may mention, that many years ago a soldier
discovered in an ancient ruined chapel on the
confines of Harris about thirty figures resembling Eastern chessmen in style and workmanship, but not in particulars. As we know that
the early Christians not only did not scruple to
employ the paraphernalia, but even made a point
of amalgamating their ceremonies with those of

the previous worship, it is not at all improbable that these images were transferred from some superseded shrine. Although apparently of Indian design, they are yet of Northern production, as they are rudely carved out of walrus tusks. Unfortunately, most of them have gone a-missing from the antiquarian museum of Edinburgh, where a few may still be seen.

Again, the symbolization, which is not necessarily the worship of the serpent, so inseparably conjoined with Buddhism as with all Sabæan mythologies—an image of the world, of eternity, as well as of life and death—is here represented at the present day.

What is the serpent-stone, so called, and employed upon so many occasions as a certain cure for all kinds of diseases? It has no resemblance whatever to the serpent, and how does it bear the name? Is it not simply a symbol of the sacred python, and a most unmistakable and widespread remnant of the primitive creed that death came by the woman, whose type is the serpent, and that through the same agency came regeneration?—as the sun, the destroyer, is the source of life. And does not this Eastern belief agree with the observation that the bite of the serpent can be best cured by the application of a piece of the reptile's skin? The serpent is burdened with the blame of ills innumerable, and is employed as a cure in the Lews either in its own person or in its symbol, this stone of simplest form and construction, which may be the whorl off their distaffs.

And here, through all these centuries of Christian rule, hidden from the priests of their received religion, this remnant of their ancient belief has remained as an ineradicable superstition, to prove the tenacious character of their Eastern intellects, and the impossibility of destroying the dwarf-palm roots of a primitive creed.

Not only is this stone employed all over the Lews and Highlands of Scotland in this way, but its exact fac-simile is a constant and widespread ornament adorning articles found amid the pre-historic remains of this country. Whether on the rude combs found in the underground

dwellings or ruined brochs, or articles of the
most varied character found in the numberless
excavations carried on in all localities, be they
apparently tumuli or unmistakably dwelling-
places, these same "ornaments" are general.
Occasionally they are in company with the
crescent moon, another type of the same idea,
showing distinctly that they were no meaning-
less representation, but that what was originally
a sacred symbol had degenerated into a Fetish.
If any doubt was felt as to its intention to represent this Sabæan symbol, its comparison with
the serpent on the Newton stone, with this peculiar figure in the centre, would surely remove it.
Here we have an unmistakable representation
of the python—the original of the symbol—so
conjoined with the symbol itself as to explain
each other: this, too, after we have just seen it
frequently conjoined with the crescent, the other
similar symbol. We have only space to add
that it has recently been discovered in Ireland,
with twelve equal divisions, as if for the Zodiac ;
while in ancient systems the serpent has been
found encircling the Zodiac (*e.g.* the Babylonian),

and has always, likewise, represented eternity and creation. Fancied analogies, says the reader. What else is all mythology?

The worship of Buddha, or a Sabæan counterpart, is so evidently symbolized in the West of Europe that even Fergusson cannot close his eyes to the fact, and endeavours to account for it by an emigration of Buddhistic tenets during times so comparatively recent as to be within the range of history. But modernists will strain at a gnat and swallow a camel. Do we not believe that all incoming creeds make the gods of the dispelled belief the evil spirits of the new? What are the evil spirits of the Gaels ycleped? *Boduchs*, pronounced Boddus, while the word still retains its ancient secondary signification of old man, head of the family, equivalent to "lord and master" in patriarchal times.

If, then, the sculptured crosses be possibly pre-Christian, this rude Lews temple of similar form may also be of ancient date. But the complete lack of figuring or sculpture does not necessitate its being of a more ancient date than those so honoured, any more than the

"Black House" in the west is more ancient than a well-built tenement in Stornoway.

Against the theory of the similarity of design of the round towers or brochs with the round towers of Ireland, it may be observed—first, the round towers cannot accommodate above a dozen people at once; then, "they are cemented by a bond of such indurated tenacity, that nothing short of lightning or earthquake has been known to disturb them;" and in these two important particulars the round towers completely differ from the Scottish dunes. These are frequently about fifty feet in diameter, and in no case that we are aware of have they ever been cemented. This might be explained in the Lews, where there is no limestone from which to form cement, and the builders might have been ignorant of the value of shell-lime so generally employed by the Culdees. But this argument has no force over many parts of the North of Scotland, where brochs are numerous.

The various collections recovered from the dunes of the mainland supply no sufficient data for any theory, although they cannot be said to point to extreme antiquity, but a time subsequent to Roman occupation. We find rude implements of flint and bone along with others of bronze and iron, clay moulds for the same, showing that they were independent of Etruscan or Phœnician " hardware merchants." Bones and horns of the reindeer are found side by side with Christian names in Roman characters, circumscribing the antiquity of the deposit. They seem to point to a semi-savage and semi-pagan population, inhabiting a rude and poor country, when " baptized men made libations of milk or beer to the demons of the place." But still they may have been for- tuitous deposits, and by no means dependent on the brochs.

If Sabæan worship ever prevailed here in its original form, it must soon have degene- rated before hordes of Scythians and Firbolgs, or equally rude Picts. These warrior races had grafted veneration for their departed chief- tains on their original sidereal creed, and, de- spising alike the delicacies of life and the ele- gancies of architecture, may have raised such semi-religious sepulchres as Callanish after the earlier and more perfect original design. "The worship of stones is among the acts of heathenism forbidden by King Edgar in the tenth, and by Cnut in the eleventh century," and possibly this historical reference pointed both to the so-called original Sabæan sculptured stones, and the ruder erections of the unlettered races that succeeded.

That such edicts are of little value may well be believed, and remains of their primary belief have possessed a powerful hold upon the people within very recent times. Thus Martin : "There is a stone in form of a cross, in the Row opposite to St. Marie's Church, about five feet high ; the natives call it the water-cross, for the ancient inhabitants had a custom of raising this sort of cross to procure rain, and when they had got enough they laid it flat on the ground." And again, Lubbock : "There was a sacred stone in Jura, round which the people used to move deasil, *i.e.* sunways. In the island of Skye, in every district, there is to be met with a rude stone consecrated to Gruagach or Apollo.

The Rev. Mr. McQueen, of Skye, says that in every village the Sun, called Grugach or the fair-haired, is represented by a rude stone; and he further states that libations of milk were poured on the Gruaich stones."

This veneration for the sun was general among them. So Martin: "In the island of Rona, off Ness, one of the natives would needs express his high esteem for my person by making a turn round about me sunways, and at the same time blessing me and wishing me all happiness."

"Also when they are got up into the island (Flannan), all of them uncover their heads, and make a turn sunways round, thanking God for their safety." "Some are very careful when they set out to sea that the boat be first rowed about sunways, and if this be neglected they are afraid their voyage may prove unfortunate."

"There was an ancient custom in the island of Lewis to make a fiery circle about the houses, corn, cattle, etc., belonging to each particular family: a man carried fire in his right hand and went round, and it was called Dessil from the right hand, which in the ancient language is called Dess." "St. Andrew's well, in the village of Shadar, is by the vulgar natives made a test to know if a sick person will die of the distemper he labours under. They send one with a wooden dish to bring some of the water to the patient, and if the dish which is then laid softly upon the surface of the water turns round sunways, they conclude that the patient will recover that distemper; but, if otherwise, that he will die." The Hyperboreans, according to Diodorus, "worship Apollo above all other gods."

Martin mentions that formerly, in cases of murrain or the plague in the Lews, all fires were extinguished and fresh fire procured by eighty-one married men rubbing two planks together until ignition followed: from the fire thus procured all the other fires were relighted afresh. So Lubbock: "The Brahman will not use ordinary fire for sacred purposes, he does not even obtain a fresh spark from flint and steel, but reverts to, or rather continues, the old way of obtaining it by friction with a wooden

drill, one Brahman pulling the string back-
wards and forwards, while another watches to
catch the sacred spark." Nine times nine is
likewise the sacred number of the Bhuddists.

From these various instances it is plain that
until recently an Eastern form of thought,
distinct from that received through Greece and
Rome, has deeply influenced the native inhabitants of the north. The Celts may have left
their Eastern cradle long prior to the rise of
any of the existing creeds, and yet the Hindoo
and the Highlander have cognate superstitions
with a common origin. We have caught
glimpses of their primitive ideas, as well as
their primitive beehive dwellings, designs, and
pottery, and may have likewise, in Callanish
and Dune Carloway, their primitive temples
and fortalices.

We have now in these two papers touched
upon a few of the antiquarian problems that
await solving in the Lews, and hope thereby
to stimulate some of our Island readers to
pursue the subject. What we require for the
elucidation of the question is, not theories,

which are abundant, but facts, which are few. Then let those who are interested in the advance of knowledge dig and investigate, with proper caution and judgment, and tell us what they find. Until we have a body of facts, theories can only be based upon sand, to be washed away by the next wave of evidence. As regards the dunes, or brochs as they are better called, Mr. Joseph Anderson, one of our ablest archæologists, holds opinion at variance with the preceding. He concludes, after abundant examination of the mainland brochs, that they were originally built by the Picts, and only thereafter taken possession of by the Norsemen. There is a similar belief current in the Lews. We require more data in support of this theory before we accept it, and meantime have grouped the Picts under Celtic Aborigines, and considered their claims as such.

But the present inhabitants are Celts, whether of Pictish or Scottish descent, and the skill with which each man erects his own unmortared stone dwelling, or helps to raise circular mills or kilns, would be natural to the descendants

of broch-builders. Just as the manufacture
of the rude "crackens" is naturally continued
to-day on the model of the ancient ware of
the brochs.

Again, it may well be that a broch is merely
a developed beehive dwelling, too large for
the builders to roof over with overlapping
stones. If this analogy were found to prevail,
it would decidedly go to disprove our Norse
theory, as no one can suppose these beehive
houses to be Scandinavian.

VIEWED generally, the animals of the Lews, as might have been expected, are all of small breed. This refers alike to wild and domesticated animals, and no doubt arises from the lack of a sufficient supply of nourishment during a great portion of the year. On the other hand, they are remarkably hardy, from constant exposure to a trying, although not a severe, climate.

The fauna is more " conspicuous by the absence" of certain classes of animals than from the presence of any peculiar to the island. No moles rear their hummocks anywhere in the country, probably the damp, peaty character of the soil neither offering a hospitable reception nor a supply of congenial food. The same may be said of rabbits, which are nowhere to be found in the Lews, although numerous in the Harris district, where the nature of the soil is more suitable. Fortunately, no rabbits means, in this instance, no foxes; so Reynard the subtle does not imitate the rich man with the pet lamb of the cotter. Hares are quite a recent addition to the animals, as the Rev. John Buchanan writes in 1790 : "There are no foxes, moles, or *hares* over all the Long Isle ; nor ferrets, partridges, black cocks, nor many of the granivorous fowls." They must have been common shortly after his time, however, as Dr. Macrae mentions " grouse, hare, and snipe " as the common game at the beginning of the century. We understand white hares were first introduced by sportsmen into Harris, whence they rapidly spread over the country. For many years they were common in the neighbouring country, but did not pass into the Uige district until the bridges were built across the Grimersta and Blackwater, and the presence in Uige of these white ghosts flitting about in the darkness created a profound impression, as the natives thought the last day must be nigh, with so many spirits going about loose. The brown hare, although common, is· not so numerous as the white mountain hare, which, however, is too easily betrayed in the brown Lews land, and is much better suited for the snow-clad slopes of Harris. They burrow in holes in the rocks, like conies, in some districts. The ferret tribe is not generally supposed to be represented, although we were informed of a large mustela (polecat ?) having been killed in the west. But we are inclined to believe there are no weasels, as we can swear to the presence of multitudes of brown rats, and a perfect plague of mice. Besides the common mouse, a specimen of the long-tailed field-mouse was brought us.

Having thus considered the negative fauna, we shall cast a rapid glance over the actual.

The cattle are of a small enduring breed, and certainly require all their peculiar powers, developed by natural selection, to starve through the long winters on little but seaware. Want

of proper feeding makes them very backward
in their growth, and a two-year-old stirk is still
a tousy-headed baby cow. They fatten well,
however, and prove sweet and excellent for the
table, bringing a large price in the English
market.

The ordinary native sheep of the cotters are
rags of creatures, manufacturing sweet mutton
out of the memory of sweet summer feeding
on the moors, and their share of the seaware.
Superior sheep have been introduced by some
of the farmers; but the best suited for the
country generally is, no doubt, the hardy
black-face, which is, at the same time, a
decided advance upon the original small native
breed.

Sheep become as active and sure-footed
as goats, scrambling about the face of the
cliffs after the sweet bits of herbage in the
crevices, their valour or hunger occasionally
outrunning their discretion and tumbling them
into the sea. On such an occasion, we have
known a daring cragsman ascend six or seven
hundred feet of sheer cliff with a dead sheep

under his arm, where several goats died of
starvation from inability to ascend.

The Barvas ponies seem a distinct species
from the Shelty, and are remarkably hardy.
They are bred principally along the stony
western district stretching from Shawbost to
Ness. To-day they have become scarce, as
their small size and great powers of endurance
cause a demand for them for coal-pits, and
the finer go for basket-carriages. They may
be seen in the ditches by the roadside up to
the knees in water, cropping the grass a foot
under the water, as if it was their most natural
position. But really none of the Lews
vertebrata could exist, if objectionably sensitive to water.

Red deer are preserved in the various
"forests," as they courteously term the tabooed
tracts of moorland, so as not to hurt the
feelings of the noble animals. They rarely
attain any size, or carry fine heads; that is to
say, the form may be good, but the antlers
even of a stag of ten are seldom considerable.
In August, 1835, Sir Frederick Johnston, who

had then the whole of the Lews shootings, shot in three weeks about one hundred head of deer. We have seen black-faced sheep much wilder than the deer in the home and Mossgiel forests.

Of the amphibia, seals and otters are both represented. The former are occasionally seen in numbers in the west; and the latter formerly inhabited almost every loch and pool. Even still they are very numerous; and as the old cotters who were most skilled in their habits, and, consequently, in their capture, are dying out, and the keepers give little attention to them, they may continue abundant. Their skins are now purchased at such a high price, however, that it will stimulate the poor to exercise their ingenuity in devising better modes for their capture.

Whales are sometimes driven on shore in multitudes by the people. Martin tells us, "Young whales are most of them eaten by the common people, who, by experience, find them to be very nourishing food. They call it sea-pork: the bigger whales are more purgative than these lesser ones, but the latter are better for nourishment." To-day they find them rather strong nourishment even for the land, unless previously made into a compost.

BIRDS.

OF birds, the eagle naturally occupies the first place, but the constant warfare waged against it by keepers, shepherds, and cotters, who have generally a few sheep, will no doubt soon exterminate it. Such a result would probably have arrived before this, if it were not that the rugged cliffs of Harris and the wilder parts of Uige afford them secure breeding-places. Even in the time of Buchanan, before 1790, he mentions that the factor, "Mr. Mackenzie, for every eagle killed in Lews gives half-a-crown;" and as the country north of Harris is flat and offers them no security, those found are generally from the west or south. Among the Barvas hills an eagle's nest was recently destroyed by letting down burning bushes from the top; and in their immediate neighbourhood we have frequently seen a pair of white sea-eagles coursing in circles.

The golden and common eagles also speed north for an occasional breakfast during the lambing season, or hover in circles about some braxy-haunted hill-side.

Of hawks, the noble peregrine falcon is the most common and most beautiful, rivalling the eagle in grace and power of flight. How often have we seen them hovering over the sea-cliffs, scaring their peculiar prey, the blue rock-pigeon, bullying the croaking ravens who dared to dispute their reign, and driving them helter-skelter to shelter ignominiously in the crevices of the rocks. You daring brigands! how the savage in our nature "cottons" to you after all!

The sparrow-hawk and the kestrel skirt the brows of the lesser eminences, and pounce upon a weaker prey. The goshawk has been shot in the west; and we were informed of a single instance of the buzzard having bred in the Uige district, but saw no specimen.

Of the brown and barn owls we saw none,

but understand they are not unknown, although the want of congenial breeding-places no doubt prevents their multiplying. The snowy owl (*Surnia nyctea*) has been frequently shot: the head-keeper procured three specimens in one morning at Ness. These large, handsome, finely marked owls may come south from Iceland or the Faroe Isles, or over from Norway.

Ravens (*Corvus corax*) are by far too numerous for the good of the cotters, farmers, and sportsmen; as their appetite for lamb requires no assistance from mint-sauce, and game-laws are as little regarded by these "blackbirds" as by Lanarkshire colliers. They have young in April, and require to place their nests in the most inaccessible rocks to escape the bold Lewis cragsman. We have dangled in vain over a sea-cliff, in our efforts to reach their eggs, the nest being unapproachable either from above or below. The grey crows (*Corvus cornix*) go in troops of twenty to fifty together, and commit many a depredation put down to the debit of the cotter children. We have known them steal the hens' eggs from about the farmyard, kill the chickens, and otherwise hang about like footpads, ready for any weak or unprotected victim that might turn up. Like all the crow race, they are far too shrewd to be readily caught napping, and, as Lewismen don't show great ingenuity in securing them, they increase and multiply to the detriment of the sportsman and the farmer. Grouse eggs, young moorfowl, chickens, or weakly birds, are at once attacked; and let but a sheep show a sign of sickness, and the proverbial "Corby picks out its een."

Rooks have been bred about the castle, eggs having been imported for this purpose, but they have not shown any attachment to the place, nor, so far as we saw, any intention to remain. We observed a flight of rooks crossing Loch Roag in September, 1871; these were probably straying from Skye or the mainland, as a large flock had been picnicing in the Uige district for some weeks before. They are said only to come with a severe gale of southeast wind, and to leave the first moderate weather, thus pointing to Skye as their home.

The rock-pigeon (*Columba livia*) is the principal representative of its family, and all around the rocky parts of the coast may be seen in great flocks, sometimes numbering several hundreds. They breed in the so-called pigeon caves everywhere plentiful, or in the numberless clefts among the rocks. As they seldom proceed far from the coast, and are always on the alert, passing like a flash from place to place, they rarely come in the way of the ordinary sportsman. The uncertainty as to their whereabouts, difficulty of approach, and their small size and little value when shot, prevent the sportsman seeking them in their haunts. Thus they increase and multiply and replenish the sea-board, forming a charming adjunct to the rude coast scenery, and only kept down by a reiving Hebridean or dashing peregrine. In the early morning we have often seen them settled among the seaware before our dwelling, feeding diligently. This was especially the case in the autumn about September. We have found their young as early as April.

A turtle-dove has been shot in the neighbourhood of Gress.

Of game birds we merely mention the names.
The red grouse (*Lagopus scoticus*) is now of more
importance in the eyes of Scottish proprietors
than the tillers of the soil. Great part of the
Lews is comparatively well stocked with them :
and, to the credit of the law-abiding people be
it said, the loss by poaching is in general
trifling.

Although the country may be said to be
well stocked with grouse, still a sportsman
need not expect to shoot his twenty or thirty
brace in a stroll before breakfast. The great
advantage of the country, indeed, to a true
sportsman, lies in the fact that he will always
get his eight to twelve brace after covering
an extensive tract of moor. The birds too
never get very wild even in November, so
that you are always sure of a fair bag after a
fair day's hard work. The ground, although
occasionally boggy, is not too trying to the
pedestrian.

No doubt this fact of the moors not carrying

too many birds, and heather never growing rank and strong, is favourable to the health of the birds, which have hitherto escaped disease to any extent.

The ptarmigan (*Lagopus vulgaris*) is shot on the hills, but is necessarily more numerous to the south. Snipes are widely distributed over the country, and, from the prevalence of marshy land, are often very numerous : like all the birds of this country, they are exquisitely tender.

The woodcock (*Scolopax rusticola*) arrives in numbers in September. Certain districts are noted for them, their habitats being exceedingly local. They have been known to breed in the island. Of the same family we have the curlew (*Numenius arquata*), everywhere abundant. Before it has taken up its permanent residence on the sea-coast, and become a little fishy, there is no more delicate bird for the table; and we consider a slice from the breast of a curlew in good condition superior in every respect to a golden plover in the short days.

The whimbrel (*Numenius phæopus*), a smaller

species of curlew, arrives sometimes in April and May in its northern migration.

The sandpiper frequents the margins of the numberless pools.

In the winter golden plover (*Charadrius pluvialis*) frequent the vicinity of the clachans in great numbers, and always, in the very shortest days, rolling in fat and in superb condition. In fine weather they retire to the more distant moors, where also they breed in summer. The dotterell (*Charadrius morinellus*) has also been shot in the west.

The lapwing (*Vanellus cristatus*) we have seen in the Uige and Barvas districts in small flocks. It only arrives in Barvas to breed, leaving immediately the young are sufficiently strong. Formerly they were in immense flocks, but are not by any means numerous to-day.

Grey herons (*Ardea cinerea*) are exceedingly common, as might be anticipated in such a land of fish-haunted pools. They are generally believed to be in best condition during full moon, when they have most success in their piscatory excursions. Their oil is con-

sidered capital for guns, and is obtained by
the primitive mode of burying them in a
manure heap, with their bill stuck in a bottle,
into which the oil distils.

The starling (*Sturnus vulgaris*) may be said
to be a Lews institution. They frequent the
whole country in large flocks, roosting in
chattering groups upon the rocks, and haunt-
ing the sea caves in myriads. We have often
amused ourselves in the evenings rolling stones
from the top of the cliffs over into some ocean
cave, to bring out the excited, and vehemently
expostulating, tenants. Around the lighthouse
at Ness are ranged rows of horsehair nooses
to catch the troublesome birds that *will* defile
the purity of the surrounding glass, that domi-
nates their rocky fastnesses. Like the pigeons
they feed among the seaware, if not also
upon it.

Another institution may be said to be the
song-thrush (*Turdus musicus*), whose name is
legion around the coast. The double intima-
tion of their presence everywhere greets the
rambler by the shore. Here, it is their ringing

song re-echoed from the cliffs; there it is the everlasting tap, tap, as they break up the shell-fish and gobble the unmailed mollusc. The destruction they caused among our bed of mussels gave some idea of the infinite quantity of shell-fish these indefatigable songsters swallow, either following the example of more highly cultivated singers, or ordered by their physician to strengthen their chests. Whenever we hear the mavis now, it recalls the cracking of the homes of the winkles, sacrificed on the altar of song.

Blackbirds (*Turdus merula*) are by no means so common, as they are a much shyer bird, and have not accommodated themselves to living in this unclad land. About the castle woods they may be found, and we have seen a few about Limshider and the west, where there is a little cover, but none are seen in the Uige district.

The fieldfare (*Turdus pilaris*) and the redwing (*T. iliacus*) arrive in the Lews in December, the former being much the more numerous.

The corncrake (*Crex pratensis*) arrives in the west in May, and during the summer we have seen more in the Lews than in any other part of the country; indeed they showed a carelessness in exposing themselves to view we have never elsewhere observed in these usually shy and retiring birds. Mr. Caunter found a corncrake alive, deep in a peat boghole, near Stornoway, in winter: no doubt it had been unable to join its comrades in their autumn migration, and may have partially hibernated. Such instances in the case of swallows have been frequent. The cuckoo also appears in May, but not in any number. Wheatears, in Lewis miscalled "Clacheran," or stonechats, adorn the top of every rock; and their note is almost as ear-monopolizing on the moor, as the thrush's by the "sad sea-shore."

The grey wagtail arrives in March.

Redbreasts have frequented the west for twenty years; but, no doubt, like the various linnets, they only date from the plantations around the castle.

The snowfleck, or snow bunting (*Plectro-*

phanes nivalis), is exceedingly common all along the roads in the winter, skipping along before the traveller ever a little further as he comes up. It is a beautifully marked little bird, and although seldom all white in this mild climate, yet shows so brightly white under the wings and on the body, as it suddenly lifts its wings in flight, that even here it well deserves its title of snowfleck. It retires into the moors to breed in the summer-time.

The wren is represented all over the country, and the golden-crested wren has been observed among the castle woods.

We have observed several specimens of a species of Hirundo, near Barvas, but have not heard of their nesting anywhere in the Lews; whether house-martins or land-martins could not be distinguished.

The wild goose (*Anser ferus*) sleeps with one eye open throughout the Lews. On the Flannan Isles it breeds in immense flocks, and often several hundred together may be seen in the Island of Pabba, on Loch Roag. They have favourite spots on the mainland where they proceed to feed, and there the ground, over a great extent, is rutted up by their strong bills, and often every sign of vegetation destroyed. If their eggs are hatched under domesticated birds, the young become quite tame, and little more given to rambling than their fellows of the farmyard. Still we have seen a flock of domesticated wild geese arrive among the domestic geese, and quietly live with them for weeks. When they gradually left, however, as leave they did, they withdrew several of the tamer ones from their allegiance, and carried them off with them, as a band of gipsies might some infatuated school-boys.

The Brent goose (*Anser Bernicla*) is also found, sometimes in immense numbers, and is still the object of popular superstition as in days of old. Thus an authority writes in 1700: "The Barnacles, or Cluk-Geese, bred in logs of wood floating on the sea, according to the common opinion, though some authors think they are bred of eggs like other fowls, but that the eggs are fastened to the logs by some glutinous matter which comes from the goose.

Those who eat of them say they taste perfectly of fir, and are certainly bred in that sort of wood." They are certainly *not* very delicate eating. Hudibras confounds them with the Solan goose.

Wild duck, teal, and widgeon, besides many others of the same family, frequent the inland lochs, and we have seen several hundred of them together on a favourite loch near Dalebeg.

The wild swan (*Cygnus ferus*) may occasionally be seen sailing majestically on some quiet inland water, singly or in pairs. They cannot be said to be frequent, as a general rule, and being far less cautious and wary than the wild goose, have not the same chance to escape either observation or destruction. We once stalked a wild swan, on a quiet loch, with the dexterity of an Indian, and, after having reached a point of vantage behind a little rising knoll, over two miles of slippery, wet, splashy, mushy moorland, raised slowly, calmly, and steadily our head and fowling-piece. There, on the calm bosom of the loch, was reflected the graceful form and pure white

swelling —— sail of a boy's boat. This was
the only time we ever saw such a thing in the
country. We reserved our fire for another
occasion, which has not yet turned up, retiring
from the field of action with all the dignity of
the fox that lost its tail.

The eider duck frequents the Flannan Isles,
where it also breeds, coming occasionally to
the western lochs of the Hebrides. On occasion of such visits it is often shot.

Goosanders (*Mergus Merganser*) are by no
means uncommon, more especially in the Uige
lochs. Their breasts are greatly sought after
for ladies' bonnets, and most deservedly so.

The great northern diver (*Colymbus glacialis*)
is everywhere common on the Atlantic coast of
the Lews. Buchanan says of it, "The Bishop
Carara, or Bunubhuachil, is larger than a
goose." The ordinary name for it is "the
bishop," and the natives aver that it retires
when old to the freshwater lochs, where it can
sustain itself more easily during the decay of its
powers. Both its relations, the black and red-
throated divers, are "companions of its solitude."

The common guillemots (*Uria troile*) are very plentiful, and quite as stupid here as elsewhere; we have shot them dozing on the waves at our door. But for interest and beauty their congenors (*Uria grylle*) the black guillemots or sea-pigeons, as they are here called, far surpass them. Of the strong elegant shape of the pigeons, their glossy black plumage, patched with white on the wings, and red legs, show them off to advantage. Alike strong on the wing and in the water, while displaying but a small surface to the action of the shot, and their close plumage throwing it readily off, they are more wary, more difficult to shoot, and more difficult to kill. These birds must cause terrible destruction amongst the fry of all kinds of fish. A common guillemot we shot in December had several hundred young sand-eels in its crop.

The razor-bill (*Utamania torda*) at certain seasons seems to supersede the black guillemot as the common object of the sea-waves, the former being more common in summer, the latter in winter.

The puffin (*Fratercula Arctica*) breeds in immense numbers in the Flannan Isles—that feathered sailors' home; but we never met a specimen straying to the mainland. Gulls are innumerable around the fishing-stations, and act as the scavengers of the sea-shore; many interesting species make night hideous with their cries during a storm.

The terns (*Sterna hirundo*) arrive about the latter end of May, when their graceful figures ever flit around the coast. Like the gulls they breed in great numbers on the small islands among the inland lochs.

The gannet or Solan goose (*Sula Bassana*) is a constant visitor, and may any day be seen turning its heels up and dropping with a splash into the sea. Or, after the general discovery of a shoal of fish, you may see these birds hurrying away with heavy wing, gorged to the beak with the successful "guzzle" their weight and size had gained them in the struggle for existence. They were formerly mentioned as one of the wonders of Scotland, from "hatching their young with one foot," but they seem to have given over those careless habits to-day.

The cormorant, scaraf, or scarf (*Phala-crocorax Carbo*) is another characteristic bird in Loch Roag. Their numbers are particularly great along this rocky, cave-haunted coast, standing on the black sea-girt rocks like sailors manning the yards. Numbers fell to our gun, and were eaten by the fishermen with relish. Their nests were made in the sea-caves and on the ledges of the high cliffs.

The green shag (*P. Graculus*), a smaller and more elegant cormorant, is also numerous, and a score of them may be seen any day taking headers into the waves as you approach some spray-girt rock. Equally at home on sea or shore, it seeks its prey at great depths in the water, and, unless shot dead, generally escapes by skill and address in diving.

In such a land the marine products, whether fish or fowl, are naturally the most liberally bestowed; and, as the Lews is primarily a huge, unwieldly, tempest-ridden fishing-station, where the shoals are, there the seafowl follow.

FISHES.

IN considering the various species of fish caught in the waters adjacent to the Lews, it may be well to premise that besides being exceedingly numerous they are of very superior excellence. Buchanan calls it "the first place in Britain for herrings and large whales, basking or sunfish, turbots, mackerels, catfish, etc." The sunfish here spoken of is the basking shark, formerly an important fishery in the west of Scotland, for the sake of its oil.

Many species which are of little value elsewhere, are firm and well-tasted here, and no one who had tasted cod from the west of the Lews would compare it with the comparatively "fushionless" fish caught in the contained lochs of the mainland.

As we do not intend to treat the subject other than generally, a simple notice of the principal fish and their habitats is all that will be given in the order of their value.

The herring of the Lews in its season is very good and of large size, but its reputation has been much injured in the market by too early fishing, before the fish is in proper condition. At one time the Loch Roag fishing in the west attracted boats from all the ports of Scotland, and was one of the most important in the country. As every loch herring has its distinctive character, the herring of Loch Roag were famous for great size and richness of quality, two hundred filling a barrel. From one of those unaccountable freaks to which this fish is given, and of which we have not been able to fathom the mystery, herring have only once appeared in quantity in this loch since the commencement of the century, although they pass round outside by Gallon Head in enormous shoals. Some attribute this to the destruction of the seaware, on which they deposited their spawn, in kelp-manufacture, but the supposition cannot apply to the numberless instances in which herring have proved as fickle in their favours as "a fair ladye." Herring are seldom quite absent from the coast, a winter fishery to a trifling extent always existing, principally for the supply of bait. At the end of April we found that herring formed the contents of the stomachs of all fish captured off the western coast. Cod, haddock, ling, and turbot, all were supplied with them, as indeed they form, when on the coast, the "harvest of the sea" to most fish. Amongst a large number of saithe and lythe caught 30th September, the saithe were in especially good condition, being full of young herring. One contained 15 of $2\frac{3}{4}$ inches long. We have observed herring fry to be most numerous along the west coast in August and September.

Sprats have occasionally been taken in quantity in Stornoway Bay.

The ling fish of this coast is unquestionably pre-eminent. We have seen one boat land a hundred fish, scarcely one under four feet long and many much over five, all in beautiful condition. They are finest and most numerous on the west and off the Butt, where they are caught in favourable seasons in incredible numbers, supplying hundreds of tons of cheap wholesome food for our large cities. A practical fisherman can tell at once from the colour whether the fish have been feeding on the far banks or in shore, and anxiously watches the success of his neighbours to know when the shoals are likely to be on his own fishing-grounds. Unlike mankind, the fish come from the West; and draw in shore towards the winter.

The cod is next in value to the ling, and is caught in much greater quantities in the Minch than in the western waters. This may partly arise from the west coast being greatly fished for cods by the English smacks, in the summer and autumn, when the Lewsmen are absent; partly from the superior value of the ling fish to the men, inducing them to select the best ground and bait for the latter.

Besides the common cod, the dorse or Baltic cod (*Callarias*) is here numerous, and in the month of May we found it was the only species brought in by the fishermen from the far banks in 50 to 60 fathoms. This shows it is generally diffused throughout these seas, as at the same time we were taking smaller specimens in-shore. They were in capital condition, while the common variety had been for some time worthless. Here they make no distinction between the two species, but as one fisherman remarked, "we consider it a good cod when it has a *chink* behind the head," which is one of its specific characteristics. We saw one about a foot long taken by the fly.

The tursk or tosk (*Brosmius vulgaris*) is perhaps the finest of the Gadidæ when fresh, being of most delicate flavour and superior to the cod. It is wholly a northern fish; with a small cat-like head, a fine buff colour, and an almost continuous fin with a black stripe running down the back and round the tail to the belly. It seldom exceeds two feet in length, and is apparently a weak fish, as it is often thrown ashore by the force of the waves. The only gastronomical objection to this delicious fish is the extra number of bones, requiring a comparative anatomist to pilot his way through.

The hake is a much inferior fish to any of those before mentioned, although by no means to be despised when fresh and well cooked. There is an extensive fishery in Stornoway Bay, and they occasionally follow the herring to the west.

Haddocks are numerous in the Minch, and occasionally found in shoals in the west. They are most voracious feeders, like all the family, and we have taken two large whelk shells containing hermit crabs, several brittle stars, and a sand eel from one. "Anything to fill up" must have been its maxim when swallowing these wretched limy starfish. Finer fish than the Lews haddocks, which frequently weigh 8 to 10 lbs. cannot be desired. Rich and delicate, firm yet tender, they are really everything that a fish, with a properly balanced mind, ought to work up to as a worthy example. Our kindest remembrances are theirs.

The whiting. This delicate fish is occasionally to be had in numbers in sheltered sea lochs, such as the inner portion of Loch Roag, where it is enticed by mussel bait. The pollack or lythe is exceedingly numerous during the summer and autumn; six to eight dozen are frequently taken in an evening by trolling. In a tideway, with the water well up and rising, and as close as possible to the rocks, you can't pull in the rod quick enough if the fish are on the feed. The young of this fish are often as brilliant in the colouring as goldfish. This occurs when they remain among the rich brown tangle, in place of coming in and out the loch with the shoal in the flow and ebb of tide. The colouring of all fish depends so much on the ground, that it is almost useless as a specific distinction; while, at the same time, it is of greater value to the fishermen as a guide to their habitats. Coal-fish are numerous in the track of the herring, and as already mentioned their progeny in the shape of "cuddies," and when more advanced as saithe, are innumerable all around the coast at certain seasons, affording an important supply of food to the inhabitants. The Loch Roag saithe are fat, firm in the flesh, and capital eating when 1½ to 2 lbs. weight.

Next in importance to the Gadidæ comes the flounder family, the various species of which are alike valuable in themselves and as bait for other victims. Of these the plaice may be said to be most numerous, and are caught in enormous quantities all round the coast to be used in the ling fisheries, for which they are favourite bait. The halibut (*Hippoglossus vulgaris*) is also caught in great numbers, and out of Stornoway is principally used as bait, although the head of a halibut of medium size is a dish to set before a king. When it weighs from 70 to 300 lbs. it becomes coarse and soft in the flesh, and is then neither suitable for bait, nor a delicacy for the table. The turbot (*Rhombus maximus*), that prince of flat-fish, is caught occasionally in numbers; but as it is not a favourite fish with the natives, from being too dry, and is most commonly cut up for bait, it is difficult to arrive at a correct knowledge of quantity or distribution. We found turbot roe fully developed on the 29th April. In the west we never paid more than a shilling for a good turbot, worth ten shillings in the Glasgow market.

Flounders (*P. flesus*) frequent the sandy bays so common around the island, and are of excellent quality; those of Broad Bay being particularly renowned.

Dabs (*P. limanda*) are also common and well-flavoured. The lemon dabs (*P. microcephalus*) are occasionally found, and are much superior in flavour and quality to the foregoing species. They are far the finest of the genus Platessa, and more resemble Rhombus both in appearance and reality. The largest we caught was sixteen inches. It was well filled with roe in March.

Muller's topknot (*Rhombus punctatus*) was only represented to our eyes in one specimen about five inches long, taken on the long lines. It seemed unknown to the fishermen, and must be exceedingly rare in these seas.

When treating of flat-fish we may remark

R

that upon Stornoway Bay being trawled by the cutter, several soles were procured. Personally we never saw one in the country, but our authority for the statement is unquestionable.

Passing on to the skates and rays we find some species exceedingly abundant. Couch affirms that they become less numerous as we proceed north, but we have seen boat after boat come in laden with them, both in the west and in Stornoway, and indeed so plentiful were they that they were selling in the latter town at 1½*d*. and even 1*d*. apiece. Weight for weight we suspect that the skate captured off the Lews would hold their own with almost any other genus, and, as they are all consumed among the natives, prove a highly important element in the daily diet of the people. The commonest species are *Raia batis*, *R. Oxyrhynchus*, and *R. clavata*, or thornback, here known as "Sonan." The first named, the blue or grey skate of the mainland, frequently come to land upwards of five feet across the wings. Their livers, rich in oil, sometimes become so buoyant as to prevent them descending should they come

to the surface, where they are secured by the
fishermen when helpless. We have seen livers
frequently 10 to 12 lbs. weight, and in one instance weighed one of 17 lbs. full of the richest
oil. Besides these species already mentioned,
R. circularis and *R. shagrinea* were observed
by us amid the spoil of the boats on the beach.

We cut an egg from *R. clavata* at the end of
March, the capsule fully formed, and filled with
yellowish matter. It would probably have been
deposited in a few days. By the way, why so
many far-fetched derivations of the word ray ?
May it not be derived from the flesh being disposed in rays, the most striking characteristic
when brought to the table ?

Among the most interesting captures in the
Lews waters is the six-gilled shark (*Notidanus
griseus*), of which Couch only mentions two
specimens as obtained hitherto on the coast of
Britain ; while at least four individuals, measur-
ing 9 to 12 feet in length, came under our own
notice. Two of these we examined. These fish
are said to be by no means uncommon here, and
are very quiet when captured, according to the

fishermen, who agree in this with Couch. Although a bottom shark they occasionally come to the surface, and a fisherman informed me he had seen one come up and bite a ling in two. They are exceedingly feeble for such large fish, and, excepting the teeth, have nothing harder than cartilage in their structure. Even the great cartilaginous jaws and vertebræ are so soft as to be cut with a knife like cheese; while the skin was also thin, soft, and pliant, but feeling rough when rubbed against the grain. At a cursory glance the most conspicuous points are—the large, open eyes, seemingly without lids, the pupils of a brilliant emerald green, brighter than the dog-fish; the distinguishing six gills; the saw-like teeth no less observable; and blunt rounded head. The larger of the two we examined measured 9 feet 4 inches long, the fluke of the tail being 2 feet 9 inches; the liver, rich in oil, weighing 52 lbs. From the weakness of the structure we were inclined to believe the fish immature, but dissection did not bear out this idea.

Specimens of the white shark (*Carcharias*)

are often brought in by the boats, but seldom
of a greater size than 4 to 6 feet in length.
That is considered quite large enough by the
men, as they fight most desperately, and are
dangerous, troublesome, and valueless captures.
These fish are mostly taken in the winter. We
were informed of a capture of a spinous shark
(*Echinorhinus spinosus*) in Stornoway Bay some
years ago. It resembled the second figure in
Yarrell, and gave several barrels of oil. The
spines being such a distinguishing characteristic, there can scarcely be any mistake as
to the species.

The picked dog-fish (*Acanthias vulgaris*) are
not numerous, but, in their season, simply
innumerable. They eat the bait, they eat the
cod and ling, they devour each other, in their
ravenous fury. They chase the capture on its
way to the boat, they wait for the bait as it
leaves the gunwale; and the whole sea
seems alive with active, indomitable, voracious
savages—like land-sharks round a silver mine,
or lawyers over the bones of a company. We
have seen a single boat throw ashore eighty

to one hundred bones of ling, nothing but the back bone left hanging to the head, as a Tartar butcher would leave the skeleton of a sheep. Even if a ling or cod be not consumed, it is ruined for the market, as the first point attacked by these pests is the liver, destroying the "amenity" of the fish. Fancy countless hordes of consumptive dogs hungering after cod-liver oil, and hunting the sea in packs to obtain it, and you have some idea of this scourge of the sea. As these viviparous fish produce their young every month, sending them into the world six to nine inches long, and able immediately to follow the rapacious habits of their parents, the breed is not likely soon to die out. Yarrell gives June to November as their breeding season, but we have found the young in numbers with the umbilical sac, dropped after the capture of the parents in March and April; and all the fishermen agree that they are found with young at all times.

The rough hound (*Squale roussette*), here named "Blind fish," from its habit of closing the eyes when captured, by drawing up the lid from below over the eye, is the only other species of dog-fish we have observed. The liver is large, and much lighter coloured than that of the picked dog. At the end of September, we found two egg-cases ready for expulsion from the Fallopian tubes, two large eggs entering the tubes, and a large quantity of eggs in all stages of development. This fish is never eaten by the people.

Gurnard, at certain seasons, take the bait freely, and the common gurnard has been known occasionally to take the fly.

Mackerel are not unknown even in considerable shoals at certain times.

Grey mullet frequent the coast more or less all the year, but are rarely captured. About Bernera, Loch Roag, they congregate in large shoals; but the fishermen do not know the English way of securing them by a false buoyed rope in front of the net.

Conger eels supply one of the principal baits for the ling fishery, but constant fishing seems to be decreasing the supply. Oil made from the fine white interior fat is considered by the natives superior to cod-liver oil.

Of the fish not sufficiently important to influence the commerce or economy of the country, the list is not so extensive as might have been expected.

The gemmeous dragonet, or gowdy (*Calliony-mus lyra*), was taken several times during our stay. One of these beautiful skulpins was nine inches long ; the head resplendent with golden yellow and streaked with fine lilac—this latter colour extending in parallel lines along its otherwise silvery sides; belly silvery. The fins, dorsal and anal, were also lined with silver and lilac, and iridescent, indeed, like the whole fish. The pectorals were delicate wing-like appendages, quite transparent. Except the plated head of its order, and the extended spine of the dorsal fin, which reaches to the end of the body, and gives the title of dragonet to the strange-looking creature, the fish is almost transparent gelatine. Gold, sapphire, and mother-of-pearl contend for pre-eminence in its composition, and its eyes are a brilliant iris, and yet this brilliant beau from the great deep is "only a gowdy" to the vulgar, and attracts no more respect than the over-dressed dandy bedizened with the splendours of Oxford Street. When fresh on the hook, it exhibits great vitality, and makes desperate and continuous exertions, its colours flashing like a prism in the sun; and it seems more like a waif from the shining Orient, than a chilly body from a chilly element in a chilly clime.

We only saw one specimen of the common skulpin (*Gieronymus Dracunculus*) taken on the spiller with lugs.

When rambling among the rocks on the shore, and diving into the treasures of the pools amid the varied algæ, the principal fish brought to light are naturally the cotti. These are numerous, and often reach large dimensions, thrusting their huge armed heads into all sorts of odd corners. The bearded rocklings, both *Motella tricirrhata* and *quinquecirrhata*, follow; the latter we have never seen longer than seven inches—when it was full of roe and evidently a mature fish. The largest *M. tricir-*

rhata we obtained, was from the Flannan Isles ; it was a very handsome fish, 15½ inches in length, and contained fragments of young lobsters, which crustacea abound there. This fish was taken in the lobster creels from upwards of twenty fathoms, and no doubt inhabits deep water ; although we do not consider with Couch that a cod, taken in forty fathoms with one in its stomach, is a proof that *tricirrhata* inhabits that depth of water. We have seen a ling liver, with a small hook quite fresh sticking in it, that must have been swallowed in twenty fathoms; while, within an hour or two, it was captured with the large hook in forty to sixty fathoms.

Gunnel fish (*Gunnellus vulgaris*) are numerous in these rocky pools, and are well named butter-fish, for slippery customers they are, and afford great amusement to the collector. The largest we procured measured 7½ inches long; and, when this size, their fins, both dorsal and anal, have very sharp spines, with which they can give a painful wound in their struggles : some were entirely free from spots. The little weevers (*Trachinus vipera*, Yar.) are most dangerous frequenters of these pools, the wound they inflict being exceedingly severe. We understand the larger weever is also found, but have never met it.

Standing on a seaweed - covered rock, the observer may frequently meet the upturned snout of the fifteen-spined stickleback (*Gasterosteus spinachia*), as it approaches to root among the seaware. This is one of the indomitable little fish that builds its nest in the forest of algæ, and defends it with constancy and courage. The only other member of the stickleback family we met with was the three-spined (*Gasterosteus spinulosus*), which we found both in the fresh and salt water lochs.

See that long seaweed in motion, while the others are scarcely influenced by the rippling waves ; how it twists and twines, as if it were a living creature! Why, it is a living creature—the strange sea-serpent, sea-kangaroo, or whatever you may please to term the family of pipe-fish (*Syngnathus*), various species of which pouch - fish glide among, and climb around, the stems of the seaware. Nature seems ever experimenting, like a chemist in his laboratory, and as frequently produces some "beautiful experiment," which is yet too delicate to bear adoption among the multifarious, rude life-manufactories. Thus these external pouches, as in the kangaroo and the penguin, have not been found compatible with the highest development among birds, animals, or fishes.

The paddle cock, or lump-sucker (*Cyclopterus lumpus*), may occasionally be found; and its masses of roe, of a beautiful pinkish tinge and firm consistency, are not uncommon on the shore. The cock has a reddish belly, and is considered good eating; but the female, which is bluish on the belly, is not made use of - here.

We were informed of the capture of a great number of John Dorys of late years, but never saw any, nor were they made use of by the people.

At Barvas a sturgeon was taken some years

ago; but it is as rare a visitant to the Hebrides as to any other portion of the kingdom. The fishermen told us they had captured a sunfish (*Orthagoriscus*, Yar.) of about 200 lbs. weight, which they had brought into Carloway Bay, and cut up for the oil-bearing liver, some years ago.

The angler, or sea-cat, as it is here called (*Lophius piscatorius*), is frequently secured. On one occasion we caught a specimen of the gluttons 2 ft. 9 in. in length, which had swallowed a conger of its own length, both coming up on the hook. The conger was still in good condition, although it had evidently been in the stomach some time, and the work of digestion seemed not to have commenced. It is indeed a most sluggish fish; and its loose, flabby skin, huge mouth, together with the stomach occupying the whole available space, point to an easy-going, gormandizing existence, supposed to be sustained by its angling appendages.

Before we leave the fishes, however, we must finish with a much more interesting fish—the

beautiful sand-launce or sand-eel, both species
of which (*Ammodytes lancea* and *A. tobianus*) are
found in quantity by those skilled in the capture.
Aided by their horny snouts, they bury themselves in the sands of the glorious Hebridean
bays, whence they may be taken by running
backward, drawing a blunted reaping-hook
through the sand. The moment it touches a
victim, the fish must be pounced upon. Tyros
either cut the eel in two, or allow it time
to escape. They are equally good as a delicacy
for the table and as a tempting bait for more
important prey, their silvery bodies showing
well in the water. In September, they formed
the only contents of the stomachs of the many
lythe we captured.

Yes! there are lots of fish in the Lews
waters, and lots of fishermen on the Lews
shores; and when energy, and capital, and
science are tired of wonderful mines at the
ends of the earth, and suicidal railways in the
middle, it will, no doubt, supply a far greater
amount of nourishment than it has yet done
to the wearied brains of our teeming cities.

HISTORICAL SKETCHES.

I.

WHETHER the earliest inhabitants of the Lews are named Dicaledones, Albanich, or Picts, it seems generally admitted that they were a pure Celtic race.

After continued inroads from the Norsemen over a lengthened period, the islands were conquered by Harald Harfager in 888. The following year they rose in rebellion, but were again crushed by a Vikingr named Ketil, who was king of the isles till his death. In 938 Aulaf Mac Sitric, son of the Danish king of Northumberland, was king of the isles; he was succeeded by Maccus Mac Arailt Mac Sitric—Gofra Mac Arailt, another king, dying in 989.

In 990 Sigurd, Earl of Orkney, conquered the Hebrides and held them through his lieutenant, Gilli. As there is mention of one Ragnal Mac Gofra, King of the Isles, who died in 1004, while Sigurd was again in possession of the isles in 1014, there is in all probability some obscurity, caused by rivals having occasionally divided the northern from the southern Hebrides, as afterwards occurred, each retaining the title of " King of the Isles."

In 1034 Earl Thorfin, son of Sigurd, reconquered the islands, which seemed to have fallen from the grasp of the Norsemen after the destructive battle of Clontarf. On his death, in 1064, they passed under the rule of an Irish prince, Diarmed Mac Maelnambo, who died in 1072. Next we find Godred, the son of Sitric, who reigned in the Isle of Man ; then his son Fingal, who was dethroned about 1077 by a Norse chieftain, Godred Crovan, son of Harald the Black. Godred Crovan was in turn expelled by the Norse king Magnus Barefoot, who placed his son Sigurd on the throne in 1093. Upon Sigurd succeeding his father as King of Norway about 1103, Lagman, son of Godred Crovan, was elected by the islanders: he afterwards died a pilgrim at Jerusalem.

Lagman was followed by a kinsman of Murchard O'Brien, King of Ireland, in 1111, who was expelled in 1113. He was succeeded by Olave the Red, youngest son of Godred Crovan, who enjoyed an unaccountably peaceable and successful reign of forty years, and was succeeded by his son, Godred the Black, in 1154. Olave's daughter Ragnhildis was married to Somerled, Prince of Argyle, and thus originated the Macdonalds, the family best known historically as Lords of the Isles. Godred the Black retained Man and the North Isles, while Somerled took possession of the South Isles. Reginald, the son of Godred the Black, was King of Man and the Isles in 1210, and it remained in the family of Godred until the death of Magnus, King of Man, in 1265.

It was in this year that the Western Isles passed from the kingdom of Norway under the allegiance of the King of Scotland; and while the remaining portions of the sub-kingdom of

S

the isles were divided among the descendants of Somerled, the Lews was conferred upon the Earl of Ross. Thus the long subjection of the Lews to Norway, extending over several centuries, ended with the cession of the Isles to Scotland in 1266.

Lewis seems to have remained in the possession of the Earls of Ross until it was confirmed by David II. to John of Isla in 1344. It thus once more became a portion of a species of sub-kingdom, which shortly afterwards comprehended all the territories formerly held by the Norse jarls, or kings, in fealty to the King of Norway. From this time the Lewis chiefs were vassals to the house of Isla.

In 1380 Donald, son of John of Isla and grandson of Robert II. by the mother's side, succeeded to his father. By marriage he claimed and secured also the earldom of Ross. In 1420 Alexander, third Lord of the Isles, entered in possession, and by the death of his mother in 1429 also became Earl of Ross. He was twice imprisoned during the life of James I. for rebellious practices, and was succeeded in 1449 by his son John. After many vicissitudes John was forfeited and deprived of his titles and estates in May, 1493; from which date the various clans which constituted his lordship, including the Macleods of Lewis, were independent of any superior but the Crown.

II.

According to Martin, Lewis is so called from "*Leog*," which, in the Irish language (Gaelic), signifies *water*. It is also derived from the Norwegian *Liod Huis*, windy house; or, following later authorities, it is Leod's Land, or land of the sons of Leod or Loyd, the eldest son of King Olave the Black, brother of Magnus, last King of Man and the Isles. Such is the received genealogy of the earliest-known chiefs. Leod's son, Torquil, was progenitor of the Lews branch, or Siol Torquil, whose possessions shortly included Rasay Island, Waterness in Skye, and Assint, Coigach, and Gairloch on the mainland.

Assint was acquired by Torquil Macleod, a

younger son of the Lews chief, who married the heiress. He was the third chief of the Lews, and a grandson of the original Torquil; and the first charter of his house was the confirmation to him of this barony by a royal grant in the reign of King David II. Previous to the Macleods, the Lews was probably held by lieutenants of the island kings; as the popular belief, that the Macnaughtons were chiefs of the Lews for three hundred years before the Macleods, seems a complete misapprehension. Indeed, it is only in the same reign in which the Macleods obtained their first charter that the Macnaughtons obtained a grant of portion of the island of Lews, when the possessions of John of the Isles were forfeited.

According to a native historian, this Torquil, the third chief, acted as conciliator between the minor chiefs of the Morrisons of Ness and the Macaulays of Uige. This would place the battle between these two small clans—which was fought near Barvas—in the thirteenth century, but would scarcely coincide with the understanding that the clan Macaulay only date from 1513. We

are also told that "the year after Torquil became chief of the Lews, he and the Macnaughton were proceeding in their birlins, or large
boats, to Stornoway, when Macleod ran the
boat of Macnaughton down in the Sound of
Jaunt, and allowed the whole crew to drown."
By this simple and effective arrangement, he
acquired an undisputed right to the whole
island, and it remained in his possession.

The next chief after Torquil was one Ruari,
whose younger son, Tormod, held Assint in
vassalage; while in 1493 his grandson, another
Ruari, whose eldest son was slain in 1481 at the
battle of the Bloody Bay, was head of the clan.
He was one of those chiefs who made their
submission to James IV. in 1494. Ruari's
second son was Torquil, who married Kathe-
rine, daughter of the first Earl of Argyle. As
Torquil was thus connected with Donald Dhu,
whose mother was also a daughter of Argyle,
he received and protected him when he escaped
from prison, and, braving forfeiture, espoused
his cause. He had previously, by a charter
under the Great Seal, been granted, in August,

1498, the office of bailliary, and eighty merks of the lands of Trotternish in Skye, on the ground of it having been formerly held by him under the Lords of the Isles. This was immediately afterwards revoked.

Although he was nominally forfeited in 1502, the combination of the island chiefs was not broken until 1506, when Torquil, as the principal remaining insurgent, was attacked in his castle at Stornoway. The castle was taken, and the whole island subjugated.

After this the Lews was restored to Malcolm, a brother of Torquil, in 1511. This Malcolm seems to have been little less turbulent than his predecessors, as we find him one of the principal adherents of Sir Donald of Lochalsh during the five years' rebellion. The Macleods of Lews and their kinsmen of Rasay also accompanied Sir Donald when he passed south to attack John Mac Ian of Ardnamurchan. They defeated the latter at Craig-an-airgid, or the Silver Craig, in Morven, slaying him and his two sons, John Sunoirtich and Angus, with many of their followers. Malcolm's second son,

Malcolm Garbh, was the progenitor of the Macleods of Rasay.

Malcolm's nephew, John, son of Torquil, who had been expressly excluded in the charter of restoration, seized the Lews on his uncle's death about 1528, and held it during his life. In 1530 he was one of the island chiefs who sent offers of submission to the king, on occasion of the rebellion of Alexander of Isla. Through a compromise with Donald Gorme, John was succeeded by his cousin, Ruari, son of Malcolm, popularly known as Old Rory. In May, 1539, Ruari, in virtue of this agreement, joined Donald Gorme in an attack upon Trotternish, in order to recover it from the Dunvegan family; but, passing over to the mainland, the expedition came to an untimely end shortly after through the death of the laird of Sleat.

Ruari first married Barbara Stewart, a daughter of Lord Methven, by whom he had one son, Torquil Eir, or the heir, to distinguish him from the succeeding sons of the same name by other wives. This son reached manhood, but perished in a storm along with 200 men,

on his way to his property of Vaternish, in
Skye. His mother died six months after his
birth, and in another half year the chief married Janet, Lady Reah, relict of the Mackay,
and daughter of the chief of Kintail.

By this second wife Ruari had another son,
Torquil, afterwards known as Torquil Connanach,
from having been reared in Strathconnan. Lady
Reah, however, eloped with a cousin of Ruari,
John Macgillechallum, of Rasay, when she
was divorced by the Lews chief, who at the
same time disowned her son, Connanach, as
being her offspring by Morrison, the Breve or
Celtic judge of the Lews. This was the occasion of a protest in 1566, taken by Donald
Gormeson, claiming to be heir of Lewis, with
the sanction of the chief, on the ground of
an alleged confession of Hugheoun, the Brew,
that Torquil Connanach was his son. Lady
Reah bore Rasay several sons and a daughter,
but, after her death, the chief and all his sons
by her were murdered by Ruari Mac Allan
Macleod, of Gerloch, brother of his second wife,
at a feast on the Island of Isay, in Waterness.

His second wife having thus eloped, Ruari married a daughter of Lauchlan Maclean, of Dowart, by whom he had two sons, Torquil Dhu and Tormad. Ruari had thus three sons named Torquil by three separate wives; the first was drowned, the third executed at Coigach by the Mackenzies; and the second, repudiated by his father, allied himself with his mother's relatives, the Mackenzies of Kintail, who used him as a catspaw to obtain possession of the Lews for themselves.

Besides these four legitimate, there were five illegitimate sons. Two of these, Tormad *Uigach* and Murdo, backed the claim of Torquil *Connanach* as heir; while three, Donald, Rory Oig, and Neil, sided with Torquil Dhu.

This old Ruari was exceedingly turbulent and lawless, offering an example which his sons were not slow to follow. In 1539 he was engaged with Donald Gorme, of Skye, against Lord Kintail, and in 1540 we find that James V. took him captive to Edinburgh, on his visit to the isles, but liberated him on giving hostages. In April, 1555, the Queen

Regent, Mary of Guise, commenced a process of treason against him, but in September of the same year he was granted a respite; and we next find him specially summoned to join the Earl of Athole, in 1565, against the insurgents under Argyle.

During the bloody disputes between Torquil *Connanach*, assisted by Kintail and Mackenzie of Gerloch, on the one hand; and Ruari, of the Lews, assisted by Donald Gorme of Sleat, Macleod of Assint, and Ruari Mac Allan, on the other, old Ruari fell into the hands of Connanach, who kept him prisoner four years. In 1572, however, before the Earl of Mar and Privy Council, he acknowledged Connanach as his son and heir, and was thereupon liberated. The turbulent chieftain was no sooner free than he revoked the deed of acknowledgment, but was again in 1576 obliged to accept Connanach as his heir, before Regent Morton and a Privy Council, bestowing upon him the district of Coigach for his maintenance.

In 1585 the feud again broke out afresh. Tormad *Uigach* was slain by Donald, who was in return captured by Murdo, but escaping seized his captor, and imprisoned him in Stornoway. Connanach now espoused the cause of his supporter, and, capturing the castle of Stornoway, again imprisoned the old Lewis chief, placing him in the castle under the custody of his son John. After a time Rory Oig retook the castle, killed Connanach's heir, and liberated old Ruari, who remained in possession till his death. Torquil, in the meantime, seized his natural brother, Donald, and executed him at Dingwall.

The piratical conduct of himself and natural sons towards all vessels touching at the Lews, was one reason for Ruari's outlawry, and gave occasion for those attempts at colonisation and civilisation made by the Fife adventurers. These attempts, as will afterwards appear, were frustrated by the combined efforts of the islanders and the Mackenzies, who looked upon the Lews as their peculiar prey.

On the death of this old freebooter, the chiefship fell to Torquil Dhu, who had married a sister of Macleod of Harris. But Connanach, aided by the Mackenzies, again invaded the Lews, took the castle of Stornoway, and, with the aid of the Morrisons of Ness, or Clann-Mhic-Ghille-Moir, secured Torquil Dhu himself. They then carried him to Coigach, in July, 1597, to ornament a tree at the end of the castle.

Torquil Dhu was chief of the Lews at the time of the expedition against the isles in 1596, when the Lews was withdrawn from the list of disobedient clans, as both Dhu and Connanach agreed to submit their claims to the authorities. The Government decided in favour of Connanach, but Torquil Dhu, who had a following of 700 to 800 men, not only kept what he previously possessed, but ravaged Coigach and Lochbroom.

Torquil Dhu having been destroyed greatly through the treachery of the Breive, who had enticed him on board a vessel at Ness, and then handed him over to Connanach, the Breive and his whole clan were attacked by Neil Macleod, and nearly extirpated. Although a Celtic institution, this Ness Brew, Breive, or Brehon, seems to have been adopted by the Norsemen, both from the name Morrison, which is Scandinavian, as well as from the fact that his jurisdiction extended over the Hebrides from Isla to the Butt of Lews, and over the opposite coast to the Ord of Caithness. This was the acknowledged Norse kingdom of the isles.

With the judge's family the records of the Lews and adjacent country were destroyed, with the exception of a few scraps carried to the mainland by some of the fugitives.

Normand or Tormad, brother of Torquil Dhu, who had long been held a prisoner by Kintail, was now liberated, that he might be the means of expelling the Fife colonists. These latter had gained a firm footing on the island, but on the appearance of the legitimate heir, the natives rose in a body under the leadership of Neil, expelled the colonists, and maintained Tormad as the leader of the Siol Torquil until 1605. In this year he gave himself up, on the return of the Fife men, and never came back to the Lews.

The antagonism of Neil Macleod, who alone remained to oppose them, at length drove the colonists out of the island; when they sold

their title to Kintail. Thus strengthened, Mackenzie was stimulated to push his claims to
the utmost. Accordingly, armed with the
deeds obtained from Torquil Connanach, whose
daughter the Tutor of Kintail, uncle of the
heir, had married, and the still better cre-
dentials of facility for invasion and pacifica-
tion, Mackenzie lost no time in securing this
extensive property. The king freed him from
all liability to other military service, that
he might direct all his force to this purpose,
seeing the purchase of the title from the Fife
adventurers had legalised Kintail's hitherto
shadowy claims. The price paid the broken
colony for their title was equal to eighty
pounds of our present money, being the estimated value of the oak woods of Letterew;
and to the woods was added permission
to erect some furnaces on the mainland
opposite.

The only resolute enemy opposed to Kintail
was Neil, the natural son of old Ruari, who
maintained an irregular warfare for some years;
but he was at length captured and induced

to proceed to Edinburgh, where he was executed.

When Cromwell's troops overran Scotland, they took possession of the Lews and fortified the whole point of Stornoway, Kintail having previously risen in rebellion. This fortification they garrisoned with fourteen hundred men! Earl Kenneth, Lord Kintail, who had always been a sincere Royalist, attacked and routed the defenders with great slaughter; but as Charles II. succeeded to the throne shortly thereafter, the Lewsmen escaped the otherwise inevitable punishment.

Although there are the remains of many ancient chapels and nunneries in the Lews, evidencing a considerable population in a comparative state of quiet, the condition of the inhabitants must have been very degraded towards the end of the possession of the Macleods. "It is told of Farquhar Macrae, born 1580, who entered the Church, that on his first visit to the island of Lews, he had to baptize the whole population under forty years of age." This points to a wretchedly disturbed state of the island during the latter end of the sixteenth century, and towards the close of old Ruari's chieftainship; while, if religion was in abeyance during these times of strife, those which followed sunk the inhabitants who remained still deeper in degeneracy. Traditions of Saxon thraldom, and Southern notions of property in land, replaced the simple ties that bound the clansman to "the head of his house." We get occasional glimpses from travellers of steady retrogression, until we arrive at the time when population was a stock to be sold with the farm, and kept down by exportation to suit the theories of the purchaser.

For a time, after the island came into the hands of the Seaforth family, little is heard of it. After the Restoration in 1660 it remained quietly in the hands of its Royalist chiefs, and although Seaforth was forfeited in 1751 for his share in the rebellion, the Lews was doubtless too distant to suffer.

The first careful account we have of the country and people is from Martin, who visited the Lews the beginning of last century, and he gives us no such hopeless account of their condition as we get from the Rev. J. Lane Buchanan, about the end of it. In Martin's time the crofters seemed comparatively well off: given to dancing, singing, and drinking home-brewed ale; and leading a free, if semi-pagan, semi-pastoral, and wholly barbarous existence. The following extract from Martin will not be out of place, seeing his work is now within the reach of few. "The inhabitants (of Long Island) had an ancient custom to sacrifice to a sea god called Shony at Hallowtide, in the manner following. The inhabitants round the Island come to the church of St. Mulvay, having each man his provision along with him. Every family furnished a peck of malt, and this was brewed into ale: one of their number was pickt out to wade into the sea up to the middle, and carrying a cup of ale in his hand standing still in that posture, cry'd out with a loud voice saying, *Shony, I give you this cup of ale, hoping that you'll be so kind as to send us plenty of seaware for enriching our ground the ensuing year;* and so threw the cup of ale

T

into the sea. This was performed in the night-time; at his return to land they all went to church, where there was a candle burning upon the altar; and then standing silent for a little time, one of them gave a signal, at which the candle was put out, and immediately all of them went to the fields, where they fell a-drinking their ale, and spent the remainder of the night in dancing, singing, &c."

The country was at this time sparsely populated, and the game, fish, and right of pasturage free to a great extent; so that, with a few acres under crop, the necessaries of life were never wanting. But the "tacksmen," or farmers, gradually extended their power, and the internal peace of the country brought its own evils. The clansmen, who had formerly to be conciliated as the military support of the chief, were now only treated as thralls to provide for his lavish expenditure. The chiefs, who were only guardians of the country for their people, gradually exercised the same proprietorship over their kinsmen as the Norman barons over their conquered Saxon dependants. Thus the tacksmen now paid heavy rental for their enlarged farms, and increased their stocks to the impoverishment of the cotters or subtenants, until abject necessity drove the latter into their power.

The Rev. John Lane Buchanan, who was intimately acquainted with the country from 1782 to 1790, writes as follows :—"It is an invariable custom, and established by a kind of tacit compact among the tacksmen and inferior lairds, to refuse, with the most invincible obstinacy, an asylum, on their ground, to any subtenant without the recommendation of his landlord, or, as he is very properly called in those parts, his *master*. The wretched outcast, therefore, has no alternative but to sink down into the situation and rank of an unfortunate and numerous class of men known under the name of *Scallags*. . . . . The scallag, whether male or female, is a poor being, who, for mere subsistence, becomes a predial slave to another, whether a subtenant, a tacksman, or a laird. The scallag builds his own hut with sods and boughs of trees; and if he is sent from one part of the country to another, he moves off his sticks, and, by means of these, forms a new hut in another place. . . . . Five days in the week he works for his master; the sixth is allowed to himself for the cultivation of some scrap of land, on the edge of some moor or mcss; on which he raises a little kail, or coleworts, barley, and potatoes. These articles, boiled up together in one mash, and often without salt, are his only food. . . . . He is allowed coarse shoes, with tartan hose, and a coarse coat, with a blanket or two for clothing." He devotes some space to a comparison between negroes on plantations and the Hebridean scallags, much to the advantage of the negro in every detail of treatment.

Again : "Formerly a Highlander would have drawn his dirk against even a laird, if he had subjected him to the indignity of a blow. At present, any tyrannical tacksman, in the absence of the laird or lord, whose presence alone can enforce good order and justice, may strike a scallag, and even a subtenant, with perfect impunity." It may be questioned whether these scallags were a recent institution, as the Celtic races of Scotland seem always to have had a race of helots subject to the free vassals!

The day of the tacksmen and sublairds did not last long. After acting as instruments in crushing out all spirit from the subtenants, they found kinship and traditional service were not reckoned when opposed to mainland gold, and none of those families whose scions formerly came back from France accomplished cavaliers can hold their places to-day.

It has been argued that the evidences of former extensive cultivation in the west of the Lews proves a considerable population; while Buchanan, on the other hand, remarks that the absence of partridges, blackcock, or many of the granivorous fowls, is a strong proof that grain has not been long sown here, and that the country has not been sufficiently cultivated to entice them to reside in it. This is scarcely an argument, as the country affords no cover

for partridge or blackcock, and only strict
preservation could secure the continued presence
even of the heath-fowl in such a populous
country. We are inclined to believe that notwithstanding emigration, enforced and otherwise, the country has been steadily advancing
in population ever since the succession of the
Mackenzies gave comparative security; while,
for a century or two before that time, the
continual wars and clan squabbles must have
sadly depopulated the land. The clergy were
driven out, the hereditary judge and his family
destroyed, and all authority, save that of the
strongest, for a time was in abeyance.

Since the beginning of the century, the
increase has been in correspondence with that
of the kingdom generally. In 1817, the population, according to Headrick, as taken by the
ground officers, was 11,534; in 1831 it had
increased to 14,541, and the latest statistics
give about 25,000.

This enormous increase in population, without
a corresponding advance in means of livelihood,
has necessarily caused a much greater number

to be little removed above pauperism. But, notwithstanding this, the condition of the people in general, as regards morality and real elements of civilisation, has infinitely improved during this century. This progress we must acknowledge to have been mainly due to the honest endeavours of the clergy, and more especially those of the Free Church of Scotland, who have reason to point with pride to the present moral character of the people under their charge. When Martin visited the island, the inhabitants were not yet emancipated from the most pagan customs.

Still later, the Rev. Mr. Buchanan gives a most deplorable account of the gross immorality of the people—viewed in the light of the accepted code—in which their ministers and elders showed them a precious example.

After describing the looseness of social ties in general, as well as in particular instances among the teachers of the people, he adds: "Presbyteries are for the most part held at public-houses, and continued sometimes without prorogation or adjournment for three successive days and nights. The holy fathers stand in no need of Paul's advice to Timothy, respecting his weak stomach. . . . . One may form a judgment of their style of living from the bill of fare for one day in Harris. This was no less than one pound sterling per head, or three pounds for the three days that the presbytery lasted. As the meetings of the presbyteries are, for the most part, scenes of riot, they are attended only by young people of both sexes, who delight in frolic." It must be added: " These are not attended with such abominable excesses as mark the clerical assemblies in some other quarters "—wherever these may be ?

In commenting upon the reverend gentleman's observations about Lewis immorality, this would partly spring from the habits and dwellings of the natives, partly from the degrading " scallag " system, and, no doubt, greatly to the freer and more primitive ideas respecting sexual intercourse always current among the Scottish lower classes.

However this may be, under the inquisitorial

rule of the Free Church clergy, the natural births have fallen to a fractional percentage ; drunkenness is rare in the country, bad language is almost never heard, and an intelligent body of people patiently submit to an arbitrary and not always intelligent control. The evil effects are, of course, those obtained under a comparatively under-educated and one-idead priesthood ; but we must be thankful for what they have really done for the social advancement of the inhabitants.

When the country passed about thirty years ago, by purchase, into the hands of Mr. Matheson, a merchant prince, all traditional devotion was destroyed. The population felt they had been purchased ; and while losing all feeling of kinship and family attachment, wholesale eviction and compulsory emigration failed to ingratiate those who remained. Thus a weird, wild song, with an infinite charm alike to native and stranger, keeps up in every " clachan " the wail of the heart-broken wanderer from the roof-tree of his love.

The tangible benefits in the shape of improved

communication do not come home to those who can race across the moor with a sack of meal on their backs, who wish nothing to be brought them, and have nothing to send away. Indeed, it is wonderful how little advantage roads are to a country as yet unsettled except around the coast, and without produce or manufactures. Cattle and sheep, like the natives, travel easier on the moors. Still, improved communication is a great boon even in a desert, and may enable some future proprietor, who shall have gone to the West, in place of the East, for his notions of government, to permanently benefit the people.

THE FIFE ADVENTURERS.

THE Lews had become so disorganized in the time of Ruari Macleod, that on his death some of the Fife barons and gentlemen resolved to secure it for colonisation, on account of its reputed fertility and valuable fisheries.

Accordingly, in 1599, they obtained the country in gift from the king, who had chosen to consider it forfeited to the Crown. The principal adventurers were the Duke of Lennox; Patrick, Commendator of Lindores; William, Commendator of Pittenweem; Sir James Anstruther, younger, of that ilk; Sir James Sandilands, of Slamanno; James Leirmonth, of Balcolmy; James Spens, of Wormestoun; John Forret, of Fingask; David Home, younger, of Wedderburne; and Captain William Murray.

These gentlemen collected a body of five to six hundred hired soldiers, besides gentlemen volunteers and artificers, with all necessaries, and sent them to the Lews, where they soon erected a small but pretty town. They were freed from any liability to rent for seven years, afterwards to be subject to a grain-rent of 140 chalders of bear (barley) for Lewis, Rona, and the Shiant Isles.

But Neil and Murdo, two of the natural sons of Old Ruari, although opposed on the question of Connanach's succession, were at one in hostility to the Fife colonists. Murdo, receiving information from Kintail, was enabled to seize the ship of the Laird of Balcolmy near the Orkneys, killing all his men, and only releasing the laird on promise of ransom, after a six months' captivity. His death on the way to Fife in 1600 prevented the fulfilment of the agreement.

Neil next attacked his brother Murdo for harbouring the Morrisons of Ness, and succeeded in capturing him, along with a number of that tribe. The Breve's relatives he killed, handing his brother Murdo over to the Fife men in exchange for a share of the island. Murdo was taken by them to St. Andrew's, and there executed, previously revealing the designs of Kintail, who had secretly employed him alike against the Fife colonists and the opponents of Connanach.

In return for his services to the colonists on this occasion, Neil received pardon at Edinburgh for his past misdeeds, and returned to the Lews with the adventurers. The prospects of the colonists now seemed so favourable, that they agreed to pay rental two years, in place of seven, after starting ; but, shortly after their return, Neil received some slight from Spens of Wormestoun, and upon the latter attempting to seize Macleod by stratagem, he was defeated with a loss of sixty men.

This seeming a propitious moment for the furtherance of his projects, Kintail introduced another element of discord by setting free Tormad, brother of Torquil Dhu, and son of old

Ruari by Maclean of Dowart's daughter.
Tormad was thus the only living acknowledged
legitimate son of old Ruari; and his appearance in the Lews, as anticipated by Kintail,
was immediately followed by his acknowledgment as chief by his natural brother Neil
and the natives.

The now-united Lewismen at once proceeded
to drive out the colonists. They attacked and
burnt the fort, killed most of the men, and
secured the commanders. These were only
liberated on condition that the king should
grant the Macleods a remission for past
offences, and that the title to the island be
delivered to Tormad Macleod. But no sooner
were the hostages at liberty, than the adventurers a third time essayed to invade the island
under the king's commission. This was de-
layed until the king was secured on the throne
of England, so that it was not till the summer
of 1605 that the Fife men once more endeavoured to secure the inhospitable island, over
which Tormad Mac Ruari had been chief since
their departure in 1601.

This expedition was so formidable, assisted as
it was by the king's ships and several Highland
gentlemen, that, against the advice of the resolute Neil, Tormad agreed to their terms and
surrendered. Proceeding to London, he placed
his legal claims before the king; but although
James received him favourably, the influence of
the adventurers was sufficient to keep him a
prisoner in Edinburgh from 1605 until 1615,
when he passed into Holland, and died in the
service of Maurice, Prince of Orange.

Neil Mac Ruari, now the only son of old
Ruari, alone remained implacable; and his
continual antagonism, together with the unfortunate results of the speculation commercially,
obliged the adventurers at length to abandon
it and return to Fife, most of them utterly
ruined thereby.

In 1608 the king again granted the island to
Lord Balmerino, Sir George Hay, and Sir James
Spens, who undertook to colonise it. In 1609
Lord Balmerino was convicted of high trea-
son; but Hay and Spens, after great prepara-
tions and assistance from the neighbouring

chiefs, re-invaded the Lews in order to plant a colony and secure the capture of the arch-rebel Neil.

Lord Kintail, on this occasion as formerly, openly assisted and countenanced the Fifemen, while he secretly thwarted the enterprise. He sent them a vessel from Ross with a supply of provisions, on which they were depending, at the same time advising Neil of its departure and destination. The latter was not slow in seizing the vessel, and the colonists, being without provisions, were forced to abandon the island, leaving a garrison only in the fort of Stornoway. The ever-active Neil again attacked and burnt the fort in 1610, sending the garrison home to Fife, from whence no colonists ever returned to endeavour to wrest the sea-encircled peat from its restless and savage occupants.

Such is the history of the well-intentioned effort to civilise the Western Isles, by planting a peaceable colony of fishermen on their then murder-haunted shores. The adventurers sank large sums of money in the enterprise, in the belief that it wuold prove to them an El Dorado, both from the believed fertility of the soil, and more especially from its wealth of fisheries. It failed, not so much from the direct hostility of the natives, headed by the brave freebooter Neil, as from the multiplicity of interests that were involved. Not only did the Mackenzies of Kintail look upon the colonists as poaching in their preserves, but the neighbouring chiefs, whose lands were alike threatened with colonisation, looked upon the cause of the Lewsmen as their own.

Thus a party of private gentlemen had to bear the brunt of the open, and still more dangerous concealed, hostility of the ruthless chiefs of the North West, all at one only in hatred of the invaders.

THE LAST OF THE MACLEODS.

AS the immediate family of old Ruari were the last of the Siol Torquil who were chiefs of the Lews, it may be interesting to trace their extirpation, for scarcely one of this restless and headstrong race seems to have died a natural death.

We have seen that Torquil Eir, the only son by the first wife, was drowned in a tempest; Torquil Connanach was disowned by his father and his title handed over to the Mackenzies; Torquil Dhu was executed by the Mackenzies, while his brother Tormad, the only remaining legitimate son, was imprisoned for ten years in Edinburgh, and only released to die in Holland. John, son of Connanach, was killed by Rory Oig, his reputed illegitimate uncle, while the three sons of Torquil Dhu, by a sister of Macleod of Harris, all died without legal issue.

Of the illegitimate sons, Normand *Uigach* was slain by his brother Donald; Murdo was handed over to the Fife men by his brother Neil, and executed at St. Andrew's; Donald was seized by Connanach and executed at Dingwall; Rory Oig, captured by Torquil Dhu, was imprisoned by Maclean, but escaped only to perish in a snow-storm.

Having thus destroyed each other like Kilkenny cats, we must follow the fortunes of the only remaining brother, Neil, who seems to have had the most ferocious energy of any of old Ruari's sons.

During his conflicts with the Fife colonists Neil had been driven out of his castle of Ness; he then took refuge on the rocky islet of Berissay, at the entrance to Loch Roag. This he strongly fortified, and from it issued periodically to harass the settlers, assisted by Macleod of Harris and others.

When the colonists had finally been driven

from the country and the titles handed over to Kintail, the latter landed with a commission of fire and sword against the turbulent islanders. The whole country was soon overrun, and the natives submitted, with the exception of Neil, who had always stubbornly opposed the pretentions of Torquil Connanach and the Mackenzies of Kintail. Retiring to his stronghold of Berissay along with Malcolm, William, and Rory—three sons of Rory Oig—Torquil Blair, and his four sons, and a following of thirty, he held it in security for three years. During this period an English pirate, named Peter Love, visited him in a vessel richly laden, and the two outlaws proposed to recapture the Lews. Love supplied Neil with guns to fortify the rock, and otherwise assisted him, while at the same time the island was well supplied with store of provisions.

It seems that the pirate had fixed his affections on a beautiful niece of Neil's, who was with him in Berissay, and a day being appointed for the marriage, Love landed with his officers and a party of his men for the festivities, while Macleod sent a body of his retainers on board the pirate vessel in order to be regaled by them in return. Such an opportunity could not be let slip, even on such an occasion, by this savage freebooter. Neil arranged previously that his flag flying on shore would be the signal that he had secured the captain and his officers, that his men on board might then capture the vessel and the intoxicated pirates. This effected, all valuables were removed and the ship set on fire.

He now sent his prisoners to Edinburgh in hopes not only of receiving the reward that had been placed on Love's head, but also of obtaining his own pardon and the liberation of his legitimate brother Tormad. For, in all the details of these ferocious times, Neil and his illegitimate brothers seem ever to have remained constant unto death in their allegiance to him they considered the rightful heir. But if Neil expected pardon he was disappointed. The pirate and his crew were hanged at Leith, and Neil and his band were no better off than before.

Their close and dangerous neighbourhood
and frequent incursions at length decided the
Mackenzies to secure them at any cost, and this
they effected eventually through an expedient
whose barbarity would have done credit to
their opponents. Assembling together all the
women and children to be found on shore
belonging to Neil and his followers, and all
in any way related to them, they placed them
on a rock opposite Berissay at ebb tide. Neil
was then notified that, unless he and his followers yielded before the return of the tide,
all who were near and dear to them would
be left at the mercy of the waves. The laments
of the women and children as the waters
advanced and threatened their destruction,
and the prospect of such a harrowing spectacle
before their eyes, were only too convincing
arguments. The ruthless desperadoes who
could feel nothing for an enemy were deeply
moved at this terrible sight, and forced most
reluctantly to deliver up the fort.

Most of his followers now submitted to the
Mackenzies; but Neil himself, with a few men,

retired into Harris under hiding, until he was forced at last to give himself up to Ruari Macleod of Harris. Macleod of Harris promised to convey him to the English king, but on the way south he was forced to yield up his prisoner to the Privy Council, along with Neil's son Donald. Neil endeavoured, with the aid of the treasure secured from the English pirate, to bribe Sir Rory to intercede on his behalf, but the catalogue of crime brought against him effectually prevented the possibility of pardon. After a life that is one long list of deeds of daring lawlessness, the robber-chief was executed on the sands of Leith, April, 1613.

His son Donald, after three years spent in England with Sir Robert Gordon, died eventually in Holland. There still remained the three sons of Rory Oig, who had been with Neil on Berissay, and who seem to have imbibed their uncle's hostility to the clan which had obtained the Lews more by fraud than right of succession. The Tutor of Kintail at length managed to seize them, when Rory and William were executed, and Malcolm was retained a prisoner. The latter, however, managed to escape, and long harassed the Mackenzies. Joining Sir James Macdonald in 1615, he made frequent incursions among the Mackenzies, and even in 1616 returned from Flanders to his shooting-ground, and killed two gentlemen of the usurping clan. He afterwards joined Sir J. Macdonald in Spain, where he remained till 1620, his further history being contained in the pregnant notice, that in 1622 and 1626 Lord Kintail and his clan were granted " commissions of fire and sword against Malcolm Mac Ruari Macleod." A worthy pendant this to the record of a race who ever " smack of the wild Norwegian," alike regardless of their own or their neighbours' lives, and dying anywhere but in their beds.

In the Lews a tale is told of the burial of the last of the race in the old church on Broad Bay, before the Mackenzies had obtained secure possession. According to the popular account, the funeral procession was on its way, when the Mackenzies appeared in force, and were about to attack the attendant Macleods. An aged islander then stepped from the *cortége*, convinced his adversaries of the folly of fighting over a dead chief, and, in exchange for freedom to deposit their honoured dead beside his stalwart ancestors, offered fealty to the invading clan. Is not a living dog better than a dead lion?

In the church of Knock, near Stornoway, may be seen the rudely sculptured figure of a warrior in a plaided kilt, with cross-hilted sword and dagger, and beneath it is popularly supposed to rest the remains of one who never knew repose in life,

THE LAST OF THE MACLEODS.

THE END.

VIRTUE AND CO., PRINTERS, CITY ROAD, LONDON.

X

"OFF THE CHAIN."

Land and Water.—The ten concluding chapters are descriptive of Islay—"Queen of the Hebrides," land of whisky, green pastures, and black cattle ; once the famed resort of the Lord of the Isles. We would gladly quote some of the author's delicious descriptions of scenery, and his quaint remarks upon things in general, peculiar to this " green isle," had we room at our disposal. We can, however, instead, strongly recommend our readers to test the author's charming style for themselves. Here and there short but very well written poems finish the chapters ; and, scattered through the 294 pages making up the volume, numerous illustrations from the author's sketches give a capital idea of the wild and picturesque beauty of the West Highland scenery. A more delightful little book than " Off the Chain " we have seldom read.

Manchester Guardian.—We have met with few books more suggestive, and, therefore, really appropriate, to the ordinary tourist. Our friend " Gowrie " has certainly some advantages which are peculiar to himself. One of these is his artistic sense. This he employs constantly, and with great profit. We have pleasure in bearing testimony to the freshness, naturalness, and vigour of his work. The sketches made in Islay are of the best in the book, and we remember no book (except the late Alexander Smith's) which smacks so racy of the soil as this. The wild grandeur of the Highlands, the rude simplicity of the Highlanders, and the truly old-world character of their lives, dwellings, and occupations are all truthfully depicted in this excellent little holiday volume.

Manchester Courier.—" Gowrie," whosoever he may be, may certainly claim credit for freshness and simplicity. He has contrived to pack into his 300 pages or so, not merely a fair quantity of lively description, but a good deal of actual information, such as is not to be obtained even by the most diligent student of guide-books and hand-books. His explorations lay chiefly in the neighbourhood of Tarbert, concerning which place and its people we get a good deal that is not only new but instructive as well. With regard to the herring fishery, he is thoroughly well informed.

Glasgow Herald.—The author, whoever he is, may be set down as a sort of universal genius or Jack-of-all-trades in literature—a man who is equally at home in metaphysics and in writing rhymes on the trawling of herring. The elephant is said to be delicate in touch as well as powerful in muscle, and, as a consequence, it can either pick up a pin or rend the gnarled oak. So it is with " Gowrie." He is at home everywhere, up to everything, and can accommodate himself to all sorts of circumstances.

Athenæum.—More than this, " Gowrie " has evidently an excellent eye for scenery. It is obvious that he travelled pleasantly and well.